Preface

The Y2K crisis involved thousands of firms and nearly every government in the world in a massive effort to head off potential system failures in computer infrastructures that were feared in the event of the date change from 1999 to 2000. In the wake of these efforts, costing hundreds of billions of dollars over several years, massive system failures did not materialize. Did the large-scale global effort prevent these failures? What are the relevant lessons from Y2K for critical infrastructure protection (CIP) more generally and where do we need to know more?

This project addressed these questions. The project was undertaken for the White House Office of Science and Technology Policy (OSTP) in order to examine the relationship of Y2K issues and concerns to CIP R&D priorities and plans. OSTP is charged under both Presidential Decision Directive 63 and the current national plan for information systems protection with coordinating the federal government's critical infrastructure protection research and development programs and plans.

The Science and Technology Policy Institute at RAND was created by Congress in 1991 as the Critical Technologies Institute and renamed in 1998. It is a federally funded research and development center sponsored by the National Science Foundation and managed by RAND. The institute's mission is to help improve public policy by conducting objective, independent research and analysis on policy issues that involve science and technology. To this end, the institute

- Supports the Office of Science and Technology Policy and other executive branch agencies, offices, and councils;

- Helps science and technology decisionmakers understand the likely consequences of their decisions and choose among alternative policies;

- Helps improve understanding in both the public and private sectors of the ways in which science and technology can better serve national objectives.

In carrying out its mission, the institute consults broadly with representatives from private industry, institutions of higher education, and other non-profit institutions.

Inquiries regarding the Science and Technology Policy Institute may be directed to the address below.

Helga Rippen
Director
Science and Technology Policy Institute

Science and Technology Policy Institute
RAND   Phone: (703) 413.1100, ext. 5351
1200 South Hayes Street   Web: http://www.rand.org/scitech/stpi
Arlington, VA 22202-5050   Email: stpi@rand.org

RAND

Concepts for Enhancing Critical Infrastructure Protection

Relating Y2K to CIP Research and Development

David Mussington

Prepared for the
Office of Science and Technology Policy

Science and Technology Policy Institute

The research described in this report was conducted by RAND's Science and Technology Policy Institute for the Office of Science and Technology Policy under Contract ENG-9812731.

Library of Congress Cataloging-in-Publication Data

Mussington, David, 1960–
    Concepts for enhancing critical infrastructure protection : relating Y2K to CIP research and development / David Mussington.
        p. cm.
    "MR-1259."
    Includes bibliographical references and index.
    ISBN 0-8330-3157-0
    1. Year 2000 date conversion (Computer systems)—United States. 2. Computer security—United States. I.Title.

QA76.76.S64 M88 2002
363,34'97—dc21

    2002024936

Published 2002 by RAND
1700 Main Street, P.O. Box 2138, Santa Monica, CA 90407-2138
1200 South Hayes Street, Arlington, VA 22202-5050
201 North Craig Street, Suite 102, Pittsburgh, PA 15213
RAND URL: http://www.rand.org/
To order RAND documents or to obtain additional information, contact Distribution Services: Telephone: (310) 451-7002; Fax: (310) 451-6915; Email: order@rand.org

Contents

Summary

"Then there was the curious incident of the dog in the nighttime."
"The dog did nothing in the nighttime."
"That was the curious incident," remarked Sherlock Holmes."

— *Silver Blaze*, the memoirs of Sherlock Holmes

Like the dog in the nighttime, the year 2000 (Y2K) crisis was puzzling because of its uneventfulness. None of the widely feared system failures materialized. Yet spending on preventive activities was hardly a non-event. According to Commerce Department estimates, the Y2K crisis cost American government and industry combined approximately $100 billion dollars between 1995 and 2001.[1] Global spending above and beyond this is hard to gauge, but an additional $100 billion is a probably a conservative estimate. Debate continues over whether the massive remediation efforts precluded catastrophic system failures or the fears were overstated to begin with. This report attempts to shed light on this debate and, by extension, examine what Y2K tells us about critical infrastructure protection (CIP) and where more knowledge is needed.

Study Purpose and Approach

This project examined the Y2K crisis and its potential to inform future efforts to protect critical infrastructures.

- What kind of event *was* the Y2K "crisis"? Was the massive and costly remediation effort justified?

- What lessons does the Y2K experience offer for CIP?

- What do these lessons imply for federal CIP research priorities?

To address these questions, the project team conducted three tasks: a literature review, focused interviews with government and industry computer experts, and a workshop involving participants in Y2K remediation efforts from industry and government. Some of the findings appear in other appended documents (the selected bibliography, the white paper presented in Appendix A, and the exercise materials presented in Appendix B). The main purpose of this report is to summarize the workshop activities and synthesize the key conclusions from all the project activities.

---

[1]Report 99-62, available at http://www.ncs.gov/n5_hp/Customer_Service/XAffairs/ NewService/NCS9962.htm.

Defining Y2K

As an event, Y2K had two main dimensions: the political/institutional dimension, which saw converging interests create unprecedented cooperation among governments and between governments and industry, and the technical dimension.

The Political/Institutional Dimension

As a political event, Y2K had a number of novel characteristics. First, both governments and the private sector perceived it as a threat to their critical information infrastructures. Second, Y2K affected systems owned by both governments and private businesses. Third, the Y2K problem was international in scope, with no single country or company immune to its effects or able to predict outcomes if neighbors suffered serious infrastructure disruptions. Taken together, these characteristics created a potential problem: remediation efforts undertaken in one sector might not be matched (or well understood) in another. In addition, differences of opinion on the likely severity of Y2K disruptions produced instances of apparent market failure, where individual enterprises lacked sufficient incentives to invest adequately in remedial measures. As hostage to the lack of remediation success of others, firms may have systematically underinvested in system vulnerability assessment and consequence management.

There was no systemwide process to allocate resources for remediation across governments or between organizations. Instead, individual organizations assessed their own vulnerability to Y2K effects, prioritized their critical systems, and undertook technical and procedural measures to mitigate potential vulnerabilities and manage risk.

Predictably, Y2K responses varied from nation to nation. Risk assessments varied, as did the mitigation efforts to address them. International organizations in the UN system (including the International Civil Aviation Organization [ICAO], the International Labor Organization [ILO], and the World Bank, to name just a few) helped to coordinate Y2K remediation activities, serving as useful channels for information sharing and lessons-learned activities. An underappreciated aspect of the Y2K response is the degree of government-to-government coordination that occurred in prioritizing key infrastructures, facilitating information sharing and remediation planning, and galvanizing public awareness by conducting consciousness-raising activities. International collaboration among states was also important for generating action in locales where skeptical governments were slow to begin remedial action. Direct bilateral appeals by the United States and other nations helped to bring even potential laggards into some sort of contingency planning and/or remediation activity.

These channels were further buttressed by the invaluable role played by multinational corporations, who propagated technical fixes for flaws discovered in critical systems. Where the economic interests of multinational corporations coincided with the economic security interests of developing countries, powerful incentives were created to make sure that no loss of critical infrastructure functionality—with its attendant negative economic impact—occurred. This fact seems to have streamlined efforts in the energy sector, for example, with multinational oil companies ensuring that partner governments were fully informed regarding the Y2K preparations undertaken at facilities within their borders. A similar phenomenon occurred in the air transportation sector, where private and public agencies in different countries shared technical and design insights on an ad hoc basis, again utilizing established institutional mechanisms to facilitate information sharing.

The Technical Dimension

Y2K was also a technical problem, though not a particularly complex one. The scale of the remediation task added a sense of urgency to the situation. The vast scale of activity required—design and implementation of software and system replacement, programming and planning for redundant system operation in case of breakdown, and deploying consequence-management programs designed to mitigate potential destructive or disruptive effects—challenged established public and private sector institutions. This activity highlighted the existing underappreciation of infrastructure interdependencies and of the potential consequences of a critical loss of services.

Was Y2K Overhyped?

The bottom-line question remains whether Y2K was overhyped or the absence of serious disruptive events validates the massive and costly remediation effort. The opinion of most informed analysts seems to be that the spending and remediation were necessary. The evidence supporting this conclusion is buried in the records of what was found when Y2K exposure analyses were undertaken in critical infrastructures. Businesses with an economic rationale for mitigating both legal liability and financial risk reached judgments that supported large expenditures to protect themselves and their suppliers from important Y2K-related difficulties. At the same time, governments throughout the world attempted to mitigate their own national risks by planning for "inevitable" disruptions, and revising civil-preparedness frameworks to manage possibly severe infrastructure collapses. Old emergency plans were dusted off, examined, and often found lacking. These plans were frequently replaced by more comprehensive inventories of vital systems and consequence-management analyses of possible disasters. Remedial technical and process measures were implemented to reduce the risk to continuity of government and public safety.

Debates over legal liability, economic cost, voluntary action versus mandates, and technical validity (of diagnoses of the Y2K problem itself) gave way to coordinated global remediation, decentralized in operation and heterogeneous in nature. Informed opinion holds that the processes and institutions responded to a common threat in a manner that successfully mitigated the potentially disastrous consequences of a unique and severe technological problem.

Lessons from Y2K for CIP

What lessons does this conclusion hold for critical infrastructure protection? Are the two problems (CIP and Y2K) similar enough to warrant the quick application of Y2K-derived institutional, process, information-sharing, and technical solutions to infrastructure protection? How context-dependent were the measures and techniques used during the Y2K remediation and consequence-management process? How vital was the U.S. government to the overall societal remediation response?

The dependence of national and economic security on critical infrastructure networks and systems is increasing in parallel with the complexity of interconnections among core networks. Technical change within the infrastructures is taking shape under imperatives driven by technological and economic forces. National security concerns may, therefore, get less attention—especially if the federal government cannot or chooses not to articulate a clear and credible threat analysis that encourages protective actions.

Private sector owners of critical infrastructures share a single overriding interest in protecting their own networks—economic survival. If threats to network functionality affect either (a) profit and loss positions or (b) legal liability for outages, they will be taken seriously. This insight was communicated to us during the interviews conducted for this project, and during the Y2K/CIP lessons learned workshop. These two concerns are further reinforced by the essential nature of many infrastructure services. Telecommunications and energy are two critical infrastructures without which much of modern life (at least in the United States) would grind to a halt. Vital services such as emergency medical and disaster response functions cannot be provided if sustained losses in energy supplies and telecommunications services occur. These concerns highlight the *public interest* in maintaining essential connectivity—an interest that is different from that which supports the flow of profits to infrastructure owners.

The technical changes that have already occurred, and that are likely to continue in critical infrastructures, rectify old vulnerabilities and flaws but also create new (and difficult to discover) ones. This means that public safety, the maintenance of vital human services, and the continuity of government argue for a significant public role in ensuring critical infrastructure protection.

Implications for CIP R&D priorities

In the context of these arguments, what sort of research and development agenda makes sense for the federal government in CIP? The agenda articulated by participants in the workshop did not differ significantly from the current federal one. National planning in this area has already established broad objectives for achieving greater knowledge and capabilities relative to both vulnerability detection and threat comprehension.

Improve Understanding of System Interdependencies

One of the most frequently identified shortfalls in knowledge related to enhancing critical infrastructure protection capabilities is the incomplete understanding of interdependencies between infrastructures. Because these interdependencies are complex, modeling efforts are commonly seen as a first step to answering persistent questions about the "real" vulnerability of infrastructures. Complex adaptive systems approaches are key to meeting this challenge and are to be recommended. However, the centrality of economics to decisions regarding the deployment of new infrastructure technologies and interconnections warrants the addition of analyses of economic criticality to the R&D agenda as a separate item. This would allow for the direct application of new research findings from the areas of network economics, complexity theory applied to macro and microeconomics, and technology and economic growth theory to the infrastructure protection issue area.

Consider CIP in a Broad Context

It is also clear that CIP is more than simply an expanded information security concern. Like Y2K, the exact concatenation of technical, political, economic, and procedural measures (not to mention sheer luck) which created the observed outcome is difficult to discern. Rather than focusing on narrow technical issues, CIP is more correctly seen as an interdisciplinary area, requiring technical, economic, public policy, legal, and national security inputs. It is logical, therefore, to propose that research be conducted in each of these areas so as to expand understanding of the national (U.S.-only) and international features of critical infrastructures which empower or retard increases in protection and information assurance.

A refocusing of CIP R&D in this manner would thus look at the following areas:

- An enhanced examination of public policy, legal, economic, and international issues in CIP

- A new focus upon economic criticality in examinations of critical infrastructure risk and consequence management.

Examine Complexity Effects

An additional area raised by complexity effects visible in both Y2K and CIP is the problem of modeling uncertainty. How can risks be adequately assessed when probabilistic techniques for estimating event/disruption distributions are not applicable? Risk management techniques and theories are therefore a near-term priority for CIP research and are closely related to the modeling of interdependencies. Modeling of vulnerabilities and risks is a vital precursor to the deployment of other techniques in protecting critical infrastructures. Without data—both real and simulated—it is unlikely that decisionmakers in either the public or private sector can be convinced to take costly decisions to enhance infrastructure protection. Metrics development, another factor closely related to infrastructure interdependency modeling, is therefore another priority.

Consider Formal Information-Sharing Processes

Information-sharing processes were not necessarily a key problem area in Y2K but have frequently been highlighted as a shortcoming in CIP. Ad hoc sharing of remediation insights and process lessons was the rule during Y2K. For CIP, it is possible that decentralized information sharing of the same type can be encouraged if the right policy, legal liability, and financial incentives are put in place by government. For R&D, government may need to create secure channels for facilitated information exchange, allowing both vulnerability *and threat* information to be more freely shared while at the same time protecting the sensitivities of both the information and provider identities. The application of XML and new database concepts to information sharing is one area where considerable commercial development is already taking place. Targeted assistance to firms developing these technologies, alongside experimental deployment of secure database and information-sharing concepts through the information-sharing and analysis centers would help to validate these concepts and enhance the informational basis for future CIP responses.

Finally, it seems that Y2K illustrated that "top-down" methods for managing information assurance are mostly, if not wholly, inappropriate for CIP. Decentralized, confederated response and information-sharing mechanisms for enhancing information assurance were not only validated by Y2K but provide a more flexible means of responding to infrastructure vulnerability. Because infrastructures are shared, information regarding vulnerabilities must also, to some extent, be shared with involved stakeholders. For CIP R&D, extensive outreach to the private sector and the academic community, the two predominant sources of both protective tools and techniques and conceptual research on infrastructure vulnerabilities, is fundamental to an effective and efficient CIP R&D strategy. In order to avoid unnecessary duplication of effort, extensive collaborative contact with outside researchers and infrastructure owners is necessary. The institutional mechanisms to bring this about already exist, with interaction between the federal government and the scientific and technical communities in established forums providing the appropriate environment for such contacts.

Concluding Observations

Y2K has much to teach us regarding the appropriate responses to CIP challenges. As demonstrated by the Y2K experience, new R&D approaches are required to deal with a complex and adaptive setting. Vulnerabilities resulting from system complexity are expanding at a much faster pace than our means of understanding them. At the same time, exploitation of infrastructure vulnerabilities for criminal, terrorist, or foreign adversary purposes is a potentially boundaryless threat. In order to bound the problem, and thereby make CIP more manageable, research is necessary to provide real data and models for understanding highly complex and uncertainty-laden environments. Our basic lack of understanding of this policy environment is the best possible rationale for a strong focus on fundamental research to enhance comprehension of networks, infrastructure interdependencies, economic criticality, and the likelihood of vulnerability exploitation (the threat). CIP R&D can make this problem more manageable. Accordingly, CIP R&D should be a high federal priority and should be pursued aggressively.

Glossary

Advisory – assessment of significant new trends or developments regarding the threat to information systems. This assessment may include analytical insights into trends, intentions, technologies, or tactics of an adversary targeting information systems.

AIS – automated information system – any equipment of an interconnected system or subsystems of equipment that is used in the automatic acquisition, storage, manipulation, control, display, transmission, or reception of data and includes software, firmware, and hardware.

Alert – notification of an event or combination of events regarding a specific attack directed at information systems.

Anomaly detection model – a model where intrusions are detected by looking for activity that is different from the user's or system's normal behavior.

Application-level gateway – (firewall) a firewall system in which service is provided by processes that maintain complete TCP connection state and sequencing. Application-level firewalls often readdress traffic so that outgoing traffic appears to have originated from the firewall, rather than the internal host.

Artificial intelligence – artificial intelligence is defined as a field of endeavor where computers and software programs are designed to mimic human reasoning and learning processes through the discovery of heuristics (rules) and algorithms that are then used to characterise an uncertain environment. Artificial intelligence-enabled systems also include those that perform at the same level as humans – utilizing other functioning mechanisms – to cope with complex environments.

ASIM – automated security incident measurement – monitors network traffic and collects information on targeted unit networks by detecting unauthorized network activity.

Assessment – surveys and inspections - an analysis of the vulnerabilities of an AIS. An information acquisition and review process designed to assist a customer to determine how best to use resources to protect information in systems.

Assurance – measure of confidence that security measures, methods, procedures, and architecture of an information system accurately mediate and enforce security policy.

ATM – asynchronous transfer mode.

ATM – automated teller machine.

Attack – an attempt to gain unauthorized access to an information system's services, resources, or information or an attempt to compromise an information system's integrity, availability, or confidentiality.

Attack tree – an analytical approach that decomposes a security target (computer, network, or complex of networks) into subsidiary parts logically and physically linked together. The links between parts, and the parts themselves, are each assumed to possess fault tolerant, neutral, or disruptive potentials that can be discerned through testing.

Authenticate – to establish the validity of a claimed user or object.

Backdoor – a hole in the security of a computer system deliberately left in place by designers or maintainers. Synonymous with trap door; a hidden software or hardware mechanism used to circumvent security measures.

Bandwidth – the amount of data that can be sent through a given communications circuit per second.

Bs7799 – British standard for information security management.

CBD-JTF – computer network defense – joint task force.

CERT – computer emergency response teams.

CGI – common gateway interface – the method that web servers use to allow interaction between servers and programs

CIP – critical infrastructure protection.

CNA – computer network attack.

Complex adaptive systems – a complex adaptive system behaves/evolves according to three key principles: order is emergent as opposed to predetermined, the system's history is irreversible, and the system's future is often unpredictable. The basic building blocks of the CAS are agents. Agents are semi-autonomous units that seek to maximize some measure of goodness, or fitness, by evolving over time.

Complexity theory – complexity theory deals with the study of systems which exhibit complex, self-organizing behavior. A complex system is any system composed of numerous parts, or agents, each of which must act individually according to its own circumstances and requirements, but which by so acting has global effects which simultaneously change the circumstances and requirements affecting all the other agents.

COTS – commercial off the shelf.

Crackers – computer experimenters and hobbyists who seek to illegally access secure and nonsecure computer networks, hardware, and software for personal financial or reputational gain.

Critical infrastructures – certain national infrastructures so vital that their incapacity or destruction would have a debilitating impact on the defense or economic security of the United States. These critical infrastructures include the information systems supporting telecommunications, electric power systems, storage and transportation of oil and natural gas, banking and finance, transportation, water supply systems, emergency services, and continuity of government.

Cryptanalysis – the analysis of a cryptographic system and/or its inputs and outputs to derive confidential variables and/or sensitive data, including clear-text.

Cryptography – the science and technology of keeping information secret from unauthorized parties by using a mathematical code or a cipher.

Defensive information operations – a process that integrates and coordinates policies and procedures, operations, personnel, and technology to protect information and defense information systems. Defensive information operations are conducted through information assurance, physical security, operations security, counterdeception, counter-psychological operations, counter-intelligence, electronic protect, and special information operations. Defensive information operations ensure timely, accurate, and relevant information access while denying adversaries the opportunity to exploit friendly information and information systems for their own purposes.

Denial-of-service attack – a network-based attack on an internet-connected world wide web, email, or access control network server – such an attack prevents users from accessing services from a targeted machine.

ECB – European Central Bank.

Fault tolerant - the ability of a *computer system* to continue to operate correctly even though one or more of its components are malfunctioning. *Note:* system performance, such as speed and *throughput,* may be diminished until the faults are corrected.

FISA – Foreign Intelligence Surveillance Act (U.S.).

FOIA – Freedom of Information Act.

GIS-enabled network monitoring systems – computer systems that use a geographical information systems interface to show the terrestrial location of an IP octet string (IP address).

Global information infrastructure (GII) – the term used to describe the convergence of local and wide area information networks fostered by the emergence of open standards in networks. Within the GII, common protocols allowing geographically separated dissimilar computer networks to interact with one another and exchange information (text, pictures, audio, or video) in a digital form. The redundant nature of the GII permits communications between networks to be routed around malfunctioning systems.

Hackers – computer hobbyists and experimenters who seek knowledge about computer systems, networks, and software for its own sake.

Incident – assessed event(s) that confirm(s) an attack on an information system. A comsec incident is an occurrence that potentially jeopardizes the security of comsec material or the secure electrical transmission of national security information or information governed by 10 U.S.C. Section 2315.

Indicator – an action or condition that might precede events detrimental to the functioning of critical infrastructures.

Information assurance – policy and procedures that protect and defend information and information systems by ensuring their availability, integrity, authentication, confidentiality, and nonrepudiation, including restoration of the information systems.

Information operations – actions taken to affect adversary information and information systems while defending one's own information and information systems.

Intelligent software agents – software programs designed to accomplish tasks independent of user intervention. In a network environment, such programs may seek out patterns in network traffic or in network usage by identifiable actors and aggregate this information into a structured presentation suitable for law enforcement use.

IRC – internet relay chat.

ISAC – information-sharing and analysis center.

ISP – internet service provider.

Money laundering – the act of transforming illegally obtained funds into legitimate financial resources integrated into the legal economy.

NIPC – National Infrastructure Protection Center (U.S.).

Node-level analysis – a process of identifying the fault tolerant, neutral, or disruptive potentials of individual subsystems within an infrastructure. Node levels are logically linked sets of nodes that allow for comparison between infrastructure systems and infrastructures which share common computing and network-connectivity characteristics.

Operations security – a process of identifying critical information and subsequently analyzing friendly actions attendant to military operations and other activities to (a) identify those actions that can be observed by adversary intelligence systems, (b) determine indicators hostile intelligence systems might obtain that could be interpreted or pieced together to derive critical information in time to be useful to adversaries, and (c) select and execute measures that eliminate or reduce to an acceptable level the vulnerabilities of friendly actions to adversary exploitation (Joint Staff, U.S. Department of Defense, Joint Publication 1-02).

Packet filter – type of firewall in which each IP packet is examined and either is allowed to pass through or is rejected, based on local security policies.

Probe – any on-line attempt to gather information about an information system or its users.

Proxy – an application acting on behalf of another application or system in responding to protocol requests.

Public-key encryption – a system of encryption utilizing a public key to authenticate the identity of an actor sending or receiving information through an encryption-enabled communications system. Public-key encryption uses separate keys to encrypt and decrypt messages meant for an authorized user. The public key is widely distributed and is used to encrypt messages meant for the public key's legitimate holder. The holder (owner of the public key) can then decrypt a message using a secret private key secure in the knowledge that the message had not been altered in transit. Public-key encryption systems also allow for the authentication of the identity of the sender in that they can be adjusted to include information regarding the identity of the sending party.

Public switched network (PSN) – the term commonly used in the U.S. telecommunications industry and elsewhere for the public telephone system.

Satcom – satellite communications.

SCADA – supervisory control and data acquisition (system) used to provide remote management capabilities for critical infrastructures such as oil and natural gas pipelines and electric power grids.

Security target – used in node-level analysis, a security target is any network, infrastructure, or computer system that may be the target of potential compromise or attack by an adversary. The security target can be decomposed into subsidiary attack targets, each of which has a discoverable level of vulnerability to known exploits, and a likelihood (probability) of assault given a known number and profile of potential attackers.

Sonet – synchronous optical network.

Spoofing – a type of attack in which the attacker steals a legitimate network address of a system and uses it to impersonate the system that owns the address. Impersonating, masquerading, mimicking, and piggybacking are all forms of spoofing.

Steganography – the art and science of communicating in a way which hides the existence of the communication.

Syn flood – a type of denial-of-service attack. It involves the alteration of data in the packet header of a TCP datagram. The altered header overflows the receiving computer's message buffer, preventing it from responding to later datagrams.

TCO – transnational criminal organization.

TCP/IP – transmission control protocol/internet protocol, the basic protocol suite, or language, underlying the interconnection of computer networks on the internet.

Threat – any circumstance or event with the potential to harm an information system through unauthorized access, destruction, disclosure, modification of data, and/or denial of service.

Usenet – internet bulletin boards including current and archived communications on particular subjects. Over 20,000 different usenet subject groups are currently active. For a survey, see http://www.deja.com.

Virtual private network (VPN) – the use of encryption over a public network to securely link two or more sites.

Vulnerability assessment – systematic examination of an information system or product to determine the adequacy of security measures, identify security deficiencies, provide data from which to predict the effectiveness of proposed security measures, and confirm the adequacy of such measures after implementation.

X.25 protocol - x.25 is a packet-switched data network protocol which defines an international recommendation for the exchange of data as well as control information between a user device (host), called *data terminal equipment* (DTE), and a network node, called *data circuit terminating equipment* (DCE).

Y2K – year 2000, an abbreviation for the year 2000 computer problem.

Acknowledgments

I am grateful for the contributions of many individuals within the U.S. government, the private sector, and RAND who helped to bring this project to a successful conclusion. First and foremost, I would like to thank the White House Office of Science and Technology Policy for sponsoring this research. My principal contact in OSTP, Lieutenant Colonel Steven Rinaldi, allowed RAND to define the scope of the project, but made highly helpful—and focusing—suggestions that kept us on track. I would also like to thank Steve's successor, Terry Kelly, for his flexibility in managing the project in its later stages.

The Y2K issue was a complex one, but the sober and clear-headed comments provided by Steve made the implementation of this research a great deal easier. Next I would like to thank my senior colleagues at RAND's Science and Technology Policy Institute. Bruce Don was instrumental in helping me define this project and provided sage advice at various points along the way. Thank you, Bruce, for your confidence and steadfastness during this lengthy enterprise.

Special thanks go to my two research assistants, Orlie Yaniv and Tracy Williams. Without their dedicated investigative work, the documentary basis for this study would have been wholly inadequate. I also want to thank Darlette Gayle for typing in the edits to the manuscript and for her skillful transcription of my barely comprehensible diagrams into something understandable to the lay and specialist reader.

A centerpiece of this project was a workshop held in June of 2000, where representatives from the government and private sector met to discuss the Y2K experience and to evaluate its meaning for critical infrastructure protection. The forthright nature of the deliberations provided me with critical insights into the composition of the risk analysis method suggested in this study and also allowed me and a number of other RAND analysts to deepen our understanding of the private and public sector dilemmas facing critical information infrastructures. Thank you to all of the participants in this workshop.

Lastly, I would like to thank my colleagues Peter Wilson and Roger Molander for providing useful feedback in the design and execution of this project. While we do not always agree on the appropriate solutions to CIP challenges, we share a common commitment to clarifying dilemmas and decisionmaking imperatives through analysis. I hope that this report contributes to this objective.

Chapter 1. Introduction

This report explores critical infrastructure protection (CIP) research and development (R&D) priorities in the context of the year 2000 (Y2K) problem. Y2K raised to prominence a number of system interdependencies, cascading failure potentials, and consequence-management problems that had been previously hidden from view. Parallel to recognition of potential Y2K problems was the growing awareness that critical infrastructures—such as electric power generation and distribution, oil and natural gas pipelines, air transportation networks, and telecommunications links—could be vulnerable to deliberate disruption by terrorists, criminals, or foreign adversaries.

Background

Presidential Decision Directive 63 (PDD 63), promulgated in May 1998, set priorities for addressing potential vulnerabilities in critical infrastructures. Among these was the drafting of remediation and recovery plans, the creation of a warning and response system, and the drafting of an intelligence collection and analysis program to provide an overview of foreign threats to critical infrastructures. PDD 63 also established research and development priorities to enhance U.S. CIP capabilities. Early efforts in this direction took place across industry, government, and academia, with the White House Office of Science and Technology Policy (OSTP) and the Critical Infrastructure Assurance Office (CIAO) serving as an important facilitator among the different entities involved.

The Y2K crisis presented an opportunity to test the recently instituted CIP plans. Activities directed at heading off major system failures took place on a massive scale, both in the U.S. and worldwide. According to Commerce Department estimates, the year 2000 (Y2K) crisis cost American government and industry combined approximately $100 billion between 1995 and 2001.[2] Global spending above and beyond this is hard to gauge, but an additional $100 billion is a probably a conservative estimate. Debate continues over whether the massive remediation efforts precluded catastrophic system failures or the fears were overstated to begin with. This report attempts to shed light on this debate,

---

[2]Report 99-62, available at http://www.ncs.gov/n5_hp/Customer_Service/XAffairs/NewService/NCS9962.htm.

examines what Y2K tells us about critical infrastructure protection, and highlights areas where more knowledge is needed.

Y2K presented those concerned with CIP a rare opportunity to evaluate concepts and information generated during work on protecting critical infrastructures. The federal government preserved only a limited amount of the data related to the foreign Y2K experience with critical infrastructures. This project contributes to this effort by focusing on R&D activities designed to mitigate long-term critical infrastructure vulnerabilities.

Project Purpose and Overview

This project was undertaken for the White House Office of Science and Technology Policy (OSTP) in order to examine the relationship of Y2K issues and concerns to CIP R&D priorities and plans. OSTP is charged under both PDD 63 and the current national plan for information systems protection with coordinating the federal government's critical infrastructure protection research and development programs and plans. OSTP responsibilities thus necessarily involve an assessment of Y2K's significance for CIP.

The research effort was launched to leverage analysis of critical infrastructure protection interdependencies against observed or feared Y2K vulnerability exposure in order to explore potential new or underresourced CIP R&D activity. In consultation with OSTP, the RAND team decided to focus on critical infrastructures in two tiers. Our criteria for this choice included the relative importance of the infrastructure to U.S. national security, the centrality of vulnerable systems to the delivery of vital government services, and finally, the importance of these infrastructures to the national economy.

The infrastructures selected for analysis are listed below.

Tier I Critical Infrastructures

- The energy sector (e.g., the electric power generation and distribution system, and the oil and gas storage and distribution system)

- The telecommunications infrastructure

- Vital human services

Tier II Critical Infrastructures

- The aviation/transportation infrastructure

- The banking and financial services infrastructure

Analysis focused primarily upon Tier I infrastructures, with the applications of Y2K/CIP linkages examined in the context of the Tier II infrastructures. This was accomplished through the careful creation of illustrative scenarios depicting Y2K failures in critical infrastructures.

The Y2K experience provided a valuable environment for evaluating the process and outputs of existing R&D resource allocation efforts in the light of revealed infrastructure interdependencies, observed failures (if any), and the overall Y2K remediation and rollover record. The project was designed to assist OSTP in capturing this valuable experiential and substantive information by:

- Identifying the potential disruptive implications of novel infrastructure interdependencies and unexpected system failures observed during Y2K on the basis of the earliest available information on both U.S. and foreign critical infrastructure disruptions

- Providing a structured workshop to evaluate established CIP R&D priorities in the context of Y2K

- Identifying potential gaps/shortfalls in existing CIP R&D priorities in the light of critical infrastructure interdependencies and other problems illuminated by the Y2K experience

- Helping to facilitate public/private sector interaction and information exchange on CIP R&D priorities in the light of the shared Y2K remediation-response-reconstitution experience.

Project Methodology

The project approached this subject by conceptualizing potential relationships between Y2K and the complex dilemmas presented by critical infrastructure protection (CIP). These concepts were linked together into a framework for examining then-current R&D priorities in CIP. The organizations charged with planning, allocating resources for, and implementing Y2K remediation tasks were frequently identical to those concerned with CIP. At the same time, many experts believed that the conceptual and analytical tools required to develop rigorous risk analysis and management perspectives for CIP were lacking.

Project Structure

The project comprised a number of mutually reinforcing elements. First, RAND generated a white paper exploring critical infrastructure protection research and development issues, which included a literature review of common themes and divergent perspectives on CIP and information security. An edited version of this paper appears as Appendix A.

A second and parallel activity was an exhaustive exploration of hypothetical explanations for the Y2K outcome. This activity—centered on two research workshops and informal discussions with a core group of experts—generated six hypotheses (or hypothetical frameworks) to explain the Y2K outcome. Due to the centrality of the second workshop to the overall project, a detailed description of its structure is given below in Chapter 2. Workshop participants were drawn from both the public and private sectors. Federal agencies were selected from among those charged with CIP responsibilities under PDD 63. Private sector representatives were selected from both large and small businesses, and from the energy and telecommunications sectors. (See Table A.1 in Appendix A for a list of the federal government agencies and infrastructure sectors represented.)

A third activity deriving from the preparation of the research workshop and the research and development white paper was the preparation of a glossary and bibliography on Y2K and CIP. These lists are presented in the front matter and following the appendices, respectively. Together, these materials constitute intermediary outputs of the project.

Workshop Design

The workshop was broken into two parts. During the first part, participants were broken into mixed (public and private sector representatives) groups and asked to deliberate on the basis of three scenario vignettes outlining potential Y2K outcomes. The list of scenarios is given below:

- Russian/Ukrainian/Polish natural gas (involved infrastructures: oil and gas storage and distribution, electric power generation and distribution)

- Italian/Central Europe financial crisis (involved infrastructures: banking and financial services, information and communications)

- North American cyber/physical terrorism (involved infrastructures: electric power generation and distribution, transportation, information and communications).

RAND *MR1259-1*

OSTP
Workshop Methodology

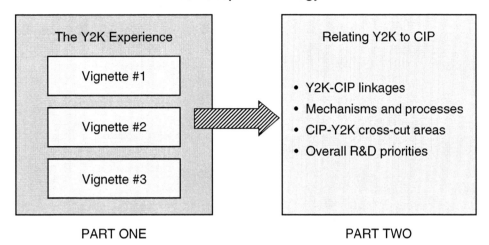

PART ONE   PART TWO

In the second part of the workshop, participants were asked to analyze the Y2K experience for potential improvements in or a refocusing of future CIP response capabilities—through the lens of potential changes in research and development priority areas.

Hypotheses

A review of literature on Y2K remediation and focused interviews conducted with officials from the federal government responsible for coordinating Y2K responses illuminated six explanatory hypotheses for the Y2K outcome. Research used to prepare the hypotheses also contributed to the design of the scenario vignettes. Both sets of materials were designed to relate to one another, allowing for a more detailed series of discussions on the validity of participant experiences of Y2K and consequence-management planning. The hypotheses, along with supporting concepts, are listed below.

Hypothesis #1 – the Y2K outcome was the result of effective remediation efforts carried out by a collaborative program involving the public and private sectors:

- Early remediation activities and last-minute fixes were both important

- Extensive information sharing took place within industry, national, and international infrastructures

- Barriers to inter- and intra-industry risk assessment on Y2K dangers were less than originally anticipated.

Hypothesis #2 – the Y2K outcome was the result of independent private sector remediation and contingency planning efforts, with minimal involvement by governments:

- Multinational corporations coordinated their activities with subsidiaries and suppliers around the world

- Industry self-interest was sufficient to galvanize collaborative private sector action even across traditionally difficult national political boundaries

- Risk assessment and remediation tools and techniques were purpose-built in the private sector and then shared on an "as-needed" basis, often at little or no cost to the user.

Hypothesis #3 – the Y2K outcome was the result of a government-led effort at energizing private sector risk assessment and technology investments in a manner that protected vital critical infrastructures from date-related disruption:

- Government anti-trust and other regulatory exemptions were important in facilitating private sector remediation

- Governmental remediation of its own systems served as an example to the broader society that the Y2K problem was considered serious, and that significant resources were being allocated to resolving it

- The creation of a central coordinating point—the President's Council for Y2K Conversion—created a focal point for governmental Y2K outreach efforts to the private sector.

Hypothesis #4 – Y2K was never a systemic threat to critical infrastructures:

- Critical infrastructures are stronger than was first thought

- Data on overseas infrastructures were incomplete, preventing an in-depth evaluation of foreign preparedness in critical systems

- The level of infrastructure interdependence was overestimated.

Hypothesis #5 – the cyber-dependence of critical infrastructures was over-estimated. Many computer-dependent infrastructures do not utilize networked support services to deliver vital operations-level functionality:

- Differences between the industrial democracies and less-developed countries were greater in this area than was appreciated, with lesser utilization of advanced control systems in poorer countries apparent

- Metrics for evaluating the effectiveness of "last minute" remediation activities were poorly developed, reducing the accuracy of prior assessments of the readiness of critical systems.

Hypothesis #6 – the Y2K outcome is inadequately explained by any of the available models of critical infrastructure protection and infrastructure interdependence:

- Infrastructure interdependencies are poorly understood, with investments in remediation being random and imitative, rather than deliberate and carefully planned

- Governmental coordination efforts seemed effective, but in the absence of a metric for understanding infrastructure interdependencies, any final judgments must be withheld.

The substantive activity that allowed participants to bridge from Y2K to CIP research and development questions was the final portion of the project methodology, the functional areas/CIP solutions matrix (see Table 1.1).

Relating Y2K Activities to CIP Research and Development

Participants were asked to take the insights gained on infrastructure interdependencies viewed from a Y2K perspective and apply them to a discussion of CIP research and development challenges. The functional areas/CIP solutions matrix was created to facilitate this activity. The questions and subject matrix summarized a set of categories where issues and concerns linking Y2K and CIP could be discussed. The matrix was composed of rows and columns, each reflecting a set of subject areas and concerns closely related to U.S. federal CIP R&D planning.

The columns in the subject matrix address areas where developments may have taken place in technical, organizational/institutional, and risk assessment categories during Y2K preparation. These categories are:

- Computing technologies – new areas of technical research illuminated by the remediation of large and complex software systems

- Tool creation – new software and hardware tools created to manage, remediate, or mitigate entirely Y2K software problems

- Information-sharing processes – new or revised information-sharing processes and channels utilized to communicate data on Y2K solutions, system or infrastructure remediation status, public and private sector shared learning on Y2K experiences

- Risk assessment models and approaches – new or revised risk assessment approaches (plans, programs, software, or methodologies) developed during the Y2K rollover.

The matrix also presents the following parallel set of functional areas derived from categories used by OSTP to coordinate the U.S. government's CIP R&D agenda:

- Threat/vulnerability/risk assessment – focuses on assessments, metrics, modeling and simulation, and test beds

- System protection – covers physical and cyber protection of individual systems; programs under this label include encryption, network security products, reliability and security of computing systems, and physical barriers

- Intrusion monitoring and response – detection and provision of immediate responses to infrastructure intrusions and attacks; programs include network intrusion detection, information assurance technologies, mobile code and agents, network defensive technologies, and explosives detection devices

Table 1.1

Potential CIP Solution/Capability Improvements

	CIP Solution Areas			
	Computing technologies (hardware and software)	Tool creation	Information-sharing processes	Risk assessment models and approaches
Functional areas				
Threat/vulnerability/ risk assessment				
System protection				
Intrusion monitoring and response				
Reconstitution				

- Reconstitution – concentrates on technologies required to reconstitute and restore critical infrastructures after serious disruptions; programs include risk management studies and tools, system survivability technologies, and consequence-management tools.

Evaluating the progress achieved during Y2K may have some applicability to ongoing CIP concerns. The matrix focused participant attention on these areas of overlap and allowed them to refine recommendations to include only those most specifically informed by the Y2K experience.

Chapter 2. The Y2K/CIP "Lessons Learned" Workshop

Introduction

The Y2K/CIP lessons learned workshop took place in June 2000 and was organized to expose experts who had analyzed or undertaken Y2K remediation projects to a range of alternate hypotheses for explaining the outcome. To this end, a selected group of specialists from the public and private sectors was assembled to discuss six explanatory hypotheses for Y2K and to examine critical infrastructure protection research and development priorities from that standpoint. The methodology and scenario vignettes used in the workshop are described in the introductory chapter. The results presented in this chapter summarize the workshop discussions—highlighting conclusions and insights gained and noting recommendations for future actions.

Y2K/CIP Deliberations

Participants were divided into three groups. These groups had identical workshop materials packages, which directed them to consider Y2K and CIP issues in a structured context.

Part One – Y2K Lessons Learned

During Part One, each of the groups deliberated on a variety of explanations for the Y2K outcome. The groups were each carefully balanced to include both public and private sector representatives. In turn, an effort was made to ensure that experienced RAND analysts were well integrated among the visitors. A key part of the activity was facilitating communication between public agencies and the private sector. In this way, information sharing could be encouraged and differences of perspective examined critically.

Participants were asked to synthesize their own Y2K experiences together with their perspectives on the scenarios presented. In doing so, group deliberations focused upon institutional, cultural, political, economic, and (of course) technical factors, which combined to produce the uniquely varied and complex Y2K events.

Group A

Focusing on information sharing, this group mentioned liability and profit motivations as important accelerators of private sector tool creation and information exchanges. In the U.S., these two areas were sufficient to engender action. The federal government's efforts to sensitize the business and international communities to the potential impact of Y2K were seen as critical catalysts in generating overseas action. The provision of "authoritative" information on Y2K status was not primarily a governmental role. Rather, private sector consultants—such as the Gartner Group—and international organizations such as the International Civil Aviation Organization (ICAO) and the International Energy Agency (IEA) served as clearinghouses for Y2K remediation information.

The U.S. government was often perceived as a market maker when it came to the provision of private sector Y2K remediation services. Once government officials went public with the potential economic and societal impact of Y2K disruptions, it was easier for private sector vendors of programming and technical services in this area to meet the growing market demand for remediation products. Governmental "consciousness raising" was a critical catalyst for those making the business case for Y2K remediation expenditures.

Group A perceived the available information on Y2K status and risks as becoming considerably clearer towards the end of 1999. Legal and institutional protections for the private sector allowed for accelerated Y2K remediation—and for public disclosures of potential risk areas. Legal liability protection was seen as a two-edged sword, however. On the one hand, this protection allowed for intra- and inter-industry information sharing on Y2K vulnerabilities and problems. At the same time, liability and indemnification measures also reduced incentives for "late starters" to actually perform Y2K remediation at all. It was unclear what the eventual balance was between these sets of incentives. The absence of significant Y2K disruptions meant that little post hoc analysis of this type was likely (or feasible).

Group participants described the dominant model of Y2K remediation within their enterprises as one of senior executive coordination, with division-level personnel implementing necessary activities. Much was made of senior company officials' awareness as an enabler for "operational" Y2K remediation activities. Public disclosures of Y2K progress seemed to allay fears that essential services and infrastructures would be unavailable in the case of an emergency.

Indeed, it appeared that as the year (1999) went on, little public upset (other than among fringe groups) was evident. This group did not offer any overall assessment of the fundamental causes of and explanations for the Y2K outcome.

Group B

Group B focused its discussions on the tremendous distrust of federal government information-sharing requests prior to Y2K. The history of private sector responses to federal government requests for information relating to computer network intrusions was raised. The FBI's bona fides were questioned and said to have poisoned the effectiveness of initial federal government policies and activities in Y2K.

Crucial enablers of public/private sector action in the case of Y2K were limitations on private sector liability for Y2K damage, anti-trust exemptions allowing industry-level exchanges of information, and the existence of a high-confidence center of information sharing in the federal government, the President's Council for Y2K chaired by John Koskinen. Transparency in the operation of federal government cross-infrastructure information sharing and communications was also a key factor that helped to build confidence. Koskinen served as a single federal "sounding board" for private sector contacts on the Y2K issue, reinforcing the federal government's ability to energize private sector remediation activities and vulnerability assessments.

Some participants noted the importance of third parties that validated the accuracy and integrity of governmental Y2K pronouncements. In this sense, the initial alarm raised by federal agencies was reinforced by industry entities perceived as sharing private sector awareness of the business requirement for continuity of operations and profitability. As such, and in contrast to Group A, Group B saw the private sector as a crucial validating actor, making credible prior governmental pronouncements on Y2K, within the industries and infrastructures involved in making fixes.

Participants also observed that the relative roles of the public and private sectors in Y2K might approximate an effective CIP response model. Basic operational/tactical information on infrastructure disruptions was seen as coming from private sector infrastructure operators. Government was seen as principally responsible for strategic (long-term and perpetrator-identifying) warning data—enabling private sector defensive and reconstitution-oriented preparations. Participants did not discuss responses above and beyond those of defensive alerts.

On a research and development point, this group felt that the government should focus on long-term research of a high-risk/high-payoff character. Tactical system integrity research in particular infrastructures (i.e., telecommunications, oil and natural gas production and distribution, electric power) were seen as the role of the private sector.

In organizational terms, Group B discussed the impact of Y2K from the standpoint of threats to business process integrity. This was seen as an effective methodological approach as it focused attention on the profit and loss impact of the interruptions in critical infrastructure-provided services and functionality. Upstream and downstream infrastructure interdependencies were seen as especially important in crafting the business case for Y2K remediation action. Granting limited Y2K liability protection and anti-trust waivers to industry acted as a catalyst for manufacturers and other businesses to contact principal suppliers and industry competitors for information on Y2K technical compliance.

As an overall assessment, Group B felt that the private sector provided the critical "on the ground" remediation of exposed systems in the U.S. The group also said that the federal government provided indispensable leadership through legislative support and relief and centralized information and coordination efforts. The "lead by example" aspect of the federal role was seen as critical to the success of joint public/private consequence-management efforts.

Noting similarities between Y2K and CIP, Group B mentioned that prioritized lessons learned from Y2K might have real meaning and value for enhancing ongoing CIP activities. Of particular note in this direction were the organizational models and information-sharing channels developed during Y2K. Participants felt that many of these mechanisms created for Y2K appeared well suited for enhancing CIP readiness. It was also observed, however, that many critical areas—such as insurance requirements for CIP preparedness, certification of information assurance measures, tools, and techniques, etc.—were still barely under development.

Group C

Group C argued that consultative mechanisms for the participation of business, government, and academia were the principal channels for Y2K information exchange. Governmentally provided information was seen as more authoritative than that gained from other sources.

Information sharing on Y2K issues prior to 1999 was seen as unproblematic. Specific information sharing in a single infrastructure appeared dependent on the amount of prior "ramp up" preparation among industry principals, or on the extent to which government focused on that sector. Overall, transparency (ease of information sharing) was seen as relatively high within infrastructures, but still only moderate between infrastructures. This latter difficulty was seen as having long-term negative consequences for CIP information sharing and lessons learned activities—even those coordinated by lead agencies.

Organizational structures for coordinating Y2K response were described as single enterprisewide coordinators, with division-level problem definition and remediation method/process selection. Frequent outsourcing of implementation measures was also described. Few incentives to share self-developed Y2K problem validation and characterization techniques were present. Multi-infrastructure applicability of remediation tools and techniques was not discussed.

Group C observed that important cross-infrastructure interdependencies were discovered during Y2K preparations. Critical interdependencies were discovered across all infrastructures, from information and communications to oil and natural gas storage and distribution. Complex infrastructure interdependencies were identified as potential sources of complex system effects in emergent vulnerabilities. Modeling and simulation approaches were seen as the best ways to increase understanding of the uncertainties involved in enhancing critical infrastructure protection.

Overall, this group felt that the Y2K outcome was predominantly explained by the effectiveness of remediation efforts carried out by the private sector, with contingency planning and recovery efforts coordinated jointly by the public and private sectors. In turn, some sectors were viewed as having mitigated most serious Y2K vulnerabilities independently of any concerted government action. As such, Y2K was a complex outcome, with a multiplicity of causal factors in evidence.

Part Two – Priority Research and Development Areas

In Part Two of the exercise, participants were asked to state their research and development priorities in the context of tools, techniques, and institutional innovations developed to manage the Y2K rollover. The priorities identified by Groups A, B, and C are listed below.

Group A: Sharing Information

- Data mining technology – applied to existing data and records of intrusions and exploits, with a view to mapping the universe of evolving CIP threats

- Development of standards – to improve computer security practices and protection levels

- Research on software and infrastructure assurance fault tolerance and quality metrics

  — Methodologies for validating CIP threat assessments

  — Tools for assessing links between CIP incidents across infrastructures and across time

  — Tools for characterizing potential critical infrastructure attack campaigns

  — Tools for assessing (interactively) absolute and relative levels of infrastructure vulnerabilities

  — Monitoring, alert, and attack assessment – information fusion and data-mining tools for the real-time assessment of computer-based attacks and/or system intrusions

  — Monitoring systems for non-cyber triggers for advanced warning of computer network attack

  — Broad spectrum key-word trigger analysis of web and usenet resources to pick up new exploits before they are used against critical infrastructure targets

  — New tool creation to make broad surveillance "sweeps" of IRC, web, and usenet resources possible

  — Visualization techniques to consolidate presentation of intrusion and exploit information on a workstation usable by system administrators.

  — Foster open-source software development for intrusion detection and system protection

Group B: Bolstering Government Trustworthiness

- Identify critical paths in infrastructures that support basic business or governmental operations – automate identification of key infrastructure resources through AI-based automated configuration management tools applied to enterprise-level systems

- Vulnerability/malicious code detection tools – to reinforce cyber-forensic capabilities

- Fiscal impact analysis/business case development tools – analysis frameworks in computer-based decision support tools for evaluating the criticality of IT resources to business/government continuity of operations

- Modeling of infrastructure interdependencies

- Automated decision support systems – based on infrastructure interdependency concepts, allowing automated responses in real time to computer network attacks such as denial-of-service incidents

- Computer-based/enhanced contingency planning and program update and testing processes for reconstitution and recovery

- Development of infrastructure and cross-infrastructure test beds to evaluate the impact of campaign-level infrastructure disruptions

Group C: Cooperative Mechanisms

- Diagnostic tools and techniques – for determining state and functionality of SCADA and other critical infrastructure systems before, during, and after critical infrastructure attacks

- Econometric models and tools for assessing the economic criticality of key national infrastructures

- Intrusion detection systems with pattern recognition and learning capabilities

- Reach beyond "signature" analysis to develop potentially dynamic profiling capabilities for detecting system intrusion

- Most likely involves development of agent-based and/or artificial intelligence technology enablers, alongside the deployment of sensors and data fusion systems to increase information quality

- Cross-infrastructure indications and warning systems

- Metrics for critical interdependencies

- Parallel organizational studies on effective models of response organization and reporting systems

- Information flow models for indications and warning across critical infrastructure boundaries

- Minimum essential information infrastructure

- Focus on an evolving definition of criticality based on economic and national security desiderata

Overlapping R&D Areas

Participants also discussed overlapping institutional and information-sharing proposals for enhancing future CIP capabilities. Among the areas identified for future conceptual and research work were:

- New methodologies for knitting together data on anomalies and "odd" system phenomena across different infrastructures

- R&D on new indications and warning concepts, new data-types and sensor modalities

- Institute for information infrastructure (I3P) organizational research into suboptimized CIP investments due to "market failure" effects

- Enablers for small business in enhancing infrastructure assurance

- Modalities for increasing infrastructure-independent research and development (IR&D) activities on computer network security

Overall Workshop Assessment

At the close of the meeting, an OSTP representative observed that the day's deliberations had been highly positive, with a number of research areas emerging that were not in the current multiyear R&D plan. The workshop raised a number of key questions that would define the future of U.S. government activity in focusing CIP R&D. These were:

- How can congressional support help to focus a coherent and comprehensive critical infrastructure protection R&D strategy in the presence of competing committee jurisdictions and stakeholder priorities?

- What answers can econometric modeling of national infrastructure criticality offer to improve contingency, reconstitution, and cross-infrastructure interdependency planning?

- What indications and warning tools and techniques can flow from the modeling and research efforts generated by Y2K to illuminate cross-sector data correlation and visualization?

These observations closed the workshop and pointed toward a future CIP R&D portfolio informed, but not driven by, insights gained from Y2K.

Chapter 3. An Analysis of the Federal CIP R&D Portfolio

Introduction

Workshop participants were asked to list their recommendations for CIP research and development priorities according to the framework described in Chapter 1. Eschewing this structure, each of the groups listed their priorities more substantively, emphasizing the relative importance of each priority, rather than adopting any external organizing typology for critical infrastructure protection research. Mapping these conclusions back into the initial framework allows for easier comparison and for the detection of clusters or gaps in research recommendations. This chapter undertakes this task.

Proposed CIP R&D Priorities

To restate the conclusions of the three groups, the research and development priorities are listed below, categorized by group and priority.

Group A

(a.1) data mining applied to CIP threat data

(a.2) CIP threat analysis methodologies

(a.3) CIP attack campaign characterization tools

(a.4) standards development

(a.5) interactive (near real-time) interdependency and risk analysis tools

(a.6) real-time network monitoring tools

(a.7) cyber/non-cyber information tools for alert, warning, and response

(a.8) visualization tools

Group B

(b.1) critical path analysis applied to IT dependence in critical infrastructures

(b.2) malicious code detection/early system vulnerability identification tools

(b.3) economic criticality analysis methodologies applied to CIP

(b.4) computer-based decision support tools for risk assessment in interdependent environments

(b.5) development of critical infrastructure interdependency models and test beds

Group C

(c.1) diagnostic tools for evaluating infrastructure systems

(c.2) economic criticality modeling of interdependent systems

(c.3) learning in intrusion detection systems (IDS) agent-based systems

(c.4) cross-infrastructure alert, warning, and response

(c.5) minimum essential information infrastructure (MEII) concepts

Reordering these priorities according to the functional areas/CIP solutions matrix advanced in Chapter 1 reveals the following arrangement of CIP research portfolios:

Federal Research Portfolio Areas	Potential CIP Solutions/Capability Improvements			
	Computing Technologies (hardware and software)	Tool Creation	Information-Sharing Processes	Risk Assessment Models and Approaches
Threat/vulnerability/risk assessment	• Critical path analysis applied to IT dependence in critical infrastructure • Malicious code detection/early system vulnerability identification tools	• Data mining applied to CIP threat data • CIP attack campaign characterization tools • Information tools for alert, warning, and response • Computer-based decision support tools for risk assessment in interdependent environments • Development of critical infrastructure interdependency models and test beds • Diagnostic tools for evaluating infrastructure systems	• Minimum essential information infrastructure (MEII) concepts	• CIP threat analysis methodologies • Critical path analysis applied to IT dependence in critical infrastructures • Computer-based decision support tools for risk assessment in interdependent environments • Minimum essential information infrastructure concepts
System protection	• Standards development, learning in IDS agent-based systems	• Interactive (near real-time) interdependency and risk analysis tools • Diagnostic tools for evaluating infrastructure systems	• Cross-infrastructure alert, warning, and response	• Interactive (near real-time) interdependency and risk analysis tools • Cross-infrastructure alert, warning, and response
Intrusion monitoring and response	• Real-time network monitoring tools			
Reconstitution	• Economic criticality analysis methodologies applied to CIP • Cross-infrastructure alert, warning, and response	• Economic criticality modeling of interdependent systems		• Critical path analysis applied to IT dependence in critical infrastructures • Economic criticality analysis methodologies applied to CIP • Economic criticality modeling of interdependent systems

Portfolio Analysis

The scope of research recommendations shows considerable overlap between groups (as represented by multiple items in different cells and by the placement of the same items in different cells). Special emphasis was placed on understanding the behavior of complex systems under stress, as demonstrated by the identification of the need for the most new tool creation in the area of threat/vulnerability/risk assessment. Risk assessment, intrusion monitoring and response, and reconstitution also emerged as important areas, with a great deal of overlap between Groups B and C in particular on this subject.

Specific technological responses for improving information sharing were relatively absent. It is not clear what accounts for this absence, but the generalized conclusion that Y2K was a transparent environment for problem solving and information dissemination may have depressed participant awareness of the parallel difficulties in CIP information sharing. As noted in Chapter 2, information-sharing channels developed for Y2K were seen as potentially useful for addressing CIP problems. The trust and transparency developed during Y2K were often described as exemplary for ongoing public/private CIP information sharing and dissemination.

In the area of system protection, participants seemed to focus on relatively well-understood topics. Research into intrusion detection systems, agent-based complex adaptive modeling of infrastructure interdependencies, and cross-infrastructure alert and warning issues (aimed at an improved appreciation of infrastructure interdependencies and possible disruption-propagation effects) is already an important part of government-sponsored research. The groups also identified the possible utility of demonstration models and test beds for joint alert, warning, and response (AWR) approaches linking different infrastructures together as an important area of work. A comparison of data from "real world" applications and simulated environments may allow for the development of increasingly sophisticated sensor and early-warning concepts useful for preprogrammed AWR responses.

In terms of novel contributions, the composite map reveals a relatively low level of emphasis on new tool creation for reconstitution (consequence management). The only entry in this cell, economic criticality modeling, was an important new addition to the research agenda. Applying economic modeling to critical infrastructure programs and plans may allow for a more quantitative approach to risk assessment and resource allocation decisions, while at the same time establishing the base for a whole new approach to resolving "market failures" in CIP provision.

Chapter 4. Conclusions

The Y2K situation produced a number of parallel interpretations of events. Participants in the Y2K/CIP lessons learned workshop reflected this multiplicity of views and indicated convergent or overlapping—as well as dissonant—understandings of the outcome during their deliberations. The conclusions presented here reflect the author's synthesis of the insights from the workshop and from the information generated during the earlier phases of the project (documented in the appendices).

Defining Y2K

As an event, Y2K has two main dimensions: the political/institutional dimension, which saw converging interests create unprecedented cooperation among governments and firms and between governments and industry; and the technical dimension.

The Political/Institutional Dimension

As a political event, Y2K has a number of novel characteristics. First, both the public and private sectors perceived Y2K as a challenge. Second, the challenge was international in scope, with no single country either immune to its effects or able to predict outcomes if neighbors suffered from serious infrastructure disruptions. Third, Y2K impacted systems owned by both governments and private businesses. These characteristics produced a potentially troublesome issue, the fact that remediation efforts in one sector would not necessarily be matched (or understood) in another. In addition, differences of opinion on the severity of the Y2K threat produced instances of apparent market failure, where the public goods aspects of Y2K remediation hindered rapid and coordinated collective efforts.

Allocation of societal resources to pay for remediation did not take place through any linear or centralized process. Rather, at the enterprise level, organizations assessed their own vulnerability and took procedural, technical, and programmatic steps to mitigate potential problems and manage risks.

Predictably, national responses to Y2K varied. Risk assessments varied, as did the integrated and resource-allocation processes designed to mitigate problems. International organizations in the UN system (including ICAO, the ILO, and the World Bank, to name just a few) helped to coordinate Y2K remediation activities, serving as a useful channel for information sharing and lessons learned fact checking. An underappreciated aspect of the Y2K response is the role that governments played in helping each other to prioritize key infrastructures, facilitate information sharing and remediation planning, and galvanize public awareness through consciousness-raising actions. International collaboration was also important to generating action in locales where governments were initially skeptical of the seriousness of the problem. Direct bilateral appeals by the United States and other nations helped to bring even potential laggards into some sort of contingency planning and/or remediation activity.

These channels were further buttressed by the invaluable role played by multinational corporations, which propagated technical fixes to flaws discovered in critical systems. Where the economic interests of multinational enterprises coincided with the national economic security imperatives of developing countries, powerful incentives were created to make sure that no loss of critical infrastructure functionality occurred. This fact seems to have streamlined efforts in the energy sector, for example, with multinational energy companies ensuring that partner governments were fully informed regarding the Y2K preparations undertaken at facilities within their borders. A similar phenomenon occurred in the air transportation sector, where private and public agencies in different countries shared technical and design insights on an ad hoc, yet structured basis, again utilizing established institutional mechanisms to facilitate information sharing.

The Technical Dimension

Y2K was also a technical problem, though not a particularly complex one. The scale of the potential remediation task provided a sense of urgency to the situation. The design and implementation of software and/or system replacement, programs and plans for redundant system operation in case of breakdown, and consequence-management programs designed to mitigate potential destructive or disruptive effects challenged established public and private sector institutions. Indeed, one of the positive aspects of Y2K may be that it exposed the lack of fundamental understanding of infrastructure interdependencies and of the consequences of a critical loss of services.

Was Y2K Overhyped?

The question remains of whether Y2K was overhyped or the absence of serious disruptive events validates decisions made to undertake remediation efforts. The opinion of most informed analysts seems to be that expenditures were necessary to make sure infrastructures functioned properly during the date change. The direct evidence supporting this conclusion, however, is buried in the records of what was found in Y2K exposure analyses undertaken in critical infrastructures throughout the world. Businesses with an economic reason for mitigating both legal liability and financial risk reached judgments that supported large expenditures to protect themselves and their suppliers from significant Y2K-related difficulties. At the same time, governments throughout the world attempted to mitigate their own national risks by planning for "inevitable" disruptions and revising civil-preparedness frameworks to better understand the possible consequences of severe infrastructure collapse. Old emergency plans were dusted off, examined, and often found lacking. These plans were frequently replaced by more comprehensive inventories of vital systems and consequence-management analyses. Remedial technical and process measures were often implemented to reduce the risk to continuity of government and public safety as a result.

Debates over legal liability, economic cost, voluntary action versus mandates, and technical validity (of diagnoses of the Y2K problem itself) gave way to a coordinated global remediation process, decentralized in operation and heterogeneous in nature. Informed public opinion is that processes and institutions responded to a common threat in a manner that successfully mitigated potentially disastrous consequences flowing from a unique and severe technological problem.

Lessons for CIP

What lessons does this conclusion hold for critical infrastructure protection responses and research? Were the two problems (CIP and Y2K) similar enough to warrant the application of Y2K-derived institutional, process, information-sharing, and technical solutions? How context-dependent were the measures and techniques used during the Y2K remediation and consequence-management process? How vital was the U.S. government to the overall societal remediation response? What does this mean for CIP R&D?

This report argues that CIP and Y2K share a core characteristic of complexity. This complexity derives from the increasing interconnection of computer network technologies linking together critical information infrastructures.

Critical infrastructure protection policymaking confronts a moving target. The dependence of national and economic security on critical infrastructures is increasing in parallel with the complex interconnection of key information systems. Technical change within critical infrastructures is taking shape under imperatives driven by technological and economic forces. National security has not, until the present, been a significant influence on infrastructure technology investment decisions. In the absence of a compelling threat analysis, a clear federal imperative for restructuring critical infrastructures to be less vulnerable to deliberate disruption was partly, if not wholly, absent.

Private sector owners of critical infrastructures share a single overriding incentive to protect their own networks—economic viability. If threats to critical infrastructure functionality impact either (a) profit and loss positions or (b) legal liability for service or functionality interruptions, they will be taken seriously. This insight was communicated to us repeatedly during the interviews conducted for this project. These two concerns are further reinforced by the essential nature of many infrastructure services. Telecommunications and energy are two critical infrastructures without which much of modern life would grind to a halt. Vital services such as emergency medical and disaster recovery functions cannot be provided if sustained losses in energy supplies and telecommunications services are suffered. These concerns create a public interest in maintaining essential connectivity separate and different from that which supports the flow of revenue to infrastructure shareholders.

Technical change brings with it solutions to historical vulnerabilities. At the same time, however, the deployment of new technologies may bring unanticipated vulnerabilities. Research into prospective vulnerabilities is a task that may exceed the private interests of business, thereby justifying prudential investments by government. Public safety, the maintenance of vital human services, and protection of national security all provide powerful rationales for a strategic effort to address critical infrastructure research priorities.

Implications for CIP R&D Priorities

What sort of research and development agenda makes sense for the federal government in CIP? The agenda articulated by workshop participants in June 2000 approximated that of the first national plan for information systems protection presented by the Clinton administration in January of that year.

Future priorities will inevitably be shaped by changing perceptions of risk and by different programmatic approaches to protecting U.S. economic and national security infrastructure assets.

Improve Understanding of System Interdependencies

One of the most frequently identified shortfalls in knowledge related to enhancing critical infrastructure protection capabilities is the incomplete understanding of interdependencies between infrastructures. Because these interdependencies are complex, modeling efforts are commonly seen as a first step to answering persistent questions about the "real" vulnerability of infrastructures. Complex adaptive systems approaches are key to meeting this challenge and are to be recommended. However, the centrality of economics to decisions regarding the deployment of new infrastructure technologies and interconnections warrants the addition of analyses of economic criticality to the R&D agenda as a separate item. This would allow for the direct application of new research findings from the areas of network economics, complexity theory applied to macro and microeconomics, and technology and economic growth theory to infrastructure protection policy development.

Consider CIP in a Broad Context

Critical infrastructure protection is a broader policy concern than narrower technical controversies over information security. As was true for Y2K, the exact concatenation of technical, political, economic, and procedural measures (not to mention sheer luck) that create a particular outcome is extremely difficult to discern. Rather than focusing on narrow technical issues, CIP is an interdisciplinary area where legal, economic, public policy, and national security inputs are fused into a single policy domain addressing vulnerabilities in critical systems. It is logical, therefore, to propose that research be conducted in each of these areas so as to expand understanding of the national and international features of critical infrastructures that empower or inhibit progress towards increased information assurance.

A refocusing of CIP R&D in this manner would thus look at the following substantive areas in greater depth:

- An enhanced examination of legal, economic, and international issues in CIP policy

- Economic criticality as an element in new assessments of critical infrastructure risk and consequence management.

Examine/Model Complexity Effects

An additional area of attention raised by the significance of complexity-related issues is that of methodologies for modeling uncertainty. How can risks be adequately assessed when probabilistic techniques for estimating event/disruption distributions are inapplicable (see Appendix A)? Risk management techniques and theories are, therefore, a near-term priority for CIP research and are closely related to the modeling of interdependencies between infrastructures. Interdependency modeling is a vital precursor to the deployment of other techniques in protecting critical infrastructures. Without data—both real and simulated—it is unlikely that decisionmakers can be convinced to take costly steps to enhance infrastructure protection. Metrics development, another factor closely related to infrastructure modeling, is therefore another priority.

Consider Formal Information-Sharing Processes

Information-sharing processes were not identified by workshop participants as a key problem area in Y2K but have frequently been named as a major shortcoming in CIP efforts. Ad hoc sharing of remediation insights and process lessons was the rule during Y2K. For CIP, it is possible that decentralized information sharing of the same type can be encouraged if the right policy, legal liability, and financial incentives are put in place by government. For R&D, government may need to create secure channels for facilitated information exchange, allowing both vulnerability and threat information to be more freely shared while at the same time protecting the sensitivities of both information and provider identities. The application of both proprietary and open-source technologies to information sharing is one area that may pay significant dividends for CIP capabilities.

Y2K illustrated that "top-down" methods of managing information assurance are unlikely to work in the CIP domain. Decentralized, confederated response and information-sharing mechanisms for enhancing information assurance are not only validated by Y2K, but provide a more flexible means of meeting a fast-changing threat to infrastructure vulnerability. Because infrastructures are shared, information sharing on vulnerabilities must also involve a multiplicity of stakeholders. For CIP R&D, extensive outreach to the private sector and the academic community, the two predominant sources of both protective tools and conceptual research in this area, is fundamental to an effective and efficient federal CIP R&D policy. To avoid unnecessary duplication of effort, extensive collaboration between scientific researchers and infrastructure operators is vital. Institutional mechanisms to foster these contacts exist, and the federal government should use its scientific research and development support to catalyze their further development.

Concluding Observations

Y2K has much to teach us regarding the appropriate responses to CIP challenges. As demonstrated by the Y2K experience, new R&D approaches are required to deal with a complex and rapidly changing vulnerability landscape. Vulnerabilities resulting from system complexity are expanding at a much faster pace than our understanding of them. Similarly, opportunities for criminal or terrorist exploitation of these infrastructure weaknesses are also expanding. It is important, then, that CIP R&D provide new tools and techniques to improve our understanding of key vulnerabilities, provide policymakers with meaningful choices in managing our risk exposure, and expand the sharing of analytical insights gained from one infrastructure to others of similar structure and criticality.

Appendix A
Evaluating the Relationship Between CIP and Y2K

Overview

Y2K and critical infrastructure protection share a number of characteristics. First, both topics address the stability and safe and secure operation of networks that deliver vital services to society and to the economy. Our growing dependence on computer networks, which form the basis of modern economic and social life, creates a potential contingent vulnerability. Disruptions in computer networks may produce economic harm. Second, and beyond the incremental losses suffered by infrastructure users (businesses, consumers, and governments), infrastructure disruptions may develop into significant threats to national security.

Fears that Y2K effects would propagate in a way threatening critical systems galvanized the U.S.—and much of the world—into multi-billion-dollar programs designed to remediate and/or replace systems discovered to be vulnerable to date-related disruptions. In turn, contingency planning, reconstitution, and recovery frameworks were created in the hope that early preparation would negate the most serious possible outcomes. Longer-term plans for lessening vulnerabilities in critical infrastructures moved in parallel to Y2K rollover efforts. The question arises then of the *transferability* of the responses created in the Y2K domain for meeting critical infrastructure protection priorities.

The Y2K non-event caused many to question the wisdom of such large investments in remediation.[1] Some argue that those with an economic interest either exaggerated the problem to sell new computer systems and software or overstated the threats to national security growing out of the rollover.

Explanations for the Y2K outcome range from those who discounted that anything would occur at all to others who see the salutary outcome as testament to the prompt and proactive action of government and the private sector working together.[2]

---

[1] See *The Foreign Y2K Experience: Lessons Learned and Implications for Critical Infrastructure* (McLean, VA: SAIC, July 31, 2000), p. 3.

[2] The General Accounting Office came to the latter conclusion in its first post-Y2K lessons learned assessment. Year 2000 computing challenge, leadership, and partnerships result in limited rollover disruptions. Statement of Joel C. Willemsen, Director, Civil Agencies Information Systems Accounting and Information Management Division, January 27, 2000. Testimony before Subcommittee on Government Management, Information and Technology, Committee on Government Reform, and the Subcommittee on Technology, Committee on Science, House of Representatives.

Relating the Y2K Outcome to Critical Infrastructure Protection: Towards an Explanatory Framework

The relationship between Y2K and CIP is both complex and largely conceptual. Programming dilemmas and remediation practices developed for Y2K may have only indirect applicability to mitigating critical infrastructure vulnerabilities. Nonetheless, any new analytical tools, system management capabilities, programming practices, and software validation techniques developed during the Y2K remediation process may still contribute longer-term capabilities for improving defensive critical infrastructure protection.

In one sense, the Y2K event was *sui generis*, in that it was a "date-certain" event, where the impacts, while of uncertain scale, were at least known in terms of their "attack vector"—that is, in terms of the types of systems that would be directly impacted. Critical infrastructure protection involves the mapping of particular vulnerabilities to *potential* exploitation by threatening actors, domestic and foreign. This appendix contrasts these two understandings in order to examine similarities and differences between Y2K exposure and critical infrastructure vulnerabilities.

To introduce the framework for understanding Y2K, the next section provides an overview of historical federal government policies and organization in CIP research and development. The priorities reflected in this policy framework could thus be used to interpret similarities with and differences from the Y2K case.

National Plan CIP R&D Priorities

As is described in the introductory chapter, PPD 63 and the draft national plan for information systems protection define a number of priority areas for CIP research.[3] Y2K remediation processes that developed tools, techniques, and procedures can be arrayed against these priorities in order to reveal the potential problem-set "overlap" between the two domains. Two questions arise at this point: What are the implications of Y2K for research and development activities in critical infrastructure protection? Are most of the behaviors, tools, organizational forms, and information-sharing channels developed for Y2K inapplicable for CIP, or are some of them "breakthroughs" that will allow for an enhancement in U.S. (and foreign) CIP capabilities? Answering these questions requires an exploration of the existing agenda of CIP R&D priorities against a structured presentation of Y2K lessons learned. Four areas characterize the current focus in the CIP R&D planning of the U.S. federal government:

1. Threat/vulnerability/risk assessment
2. System protection

---

[3] This document draws upon *Defending America's Cyberspace: National Plan for Information Systems Protection*, version 1.0, January 2000, for its description of policy as it existed during the Y2K rollover. The Bush administration significantly modified this framework following policy reviews and institutional changes in the summer of 2001.

3. Intrusion monitoring and response

4. Reconstitution

Federal departments have been designated to serve as lead agencies charged with CIP response planning and outreach to the private sector in infrastructure protection plans. These assignments also convey R&D responsibilities with respect to CIP vulnerabilities and issues relating to particular infrastructures. These assignments are listed in Table A.1.

able

CP Lea   gencies

Critical Infrastructure Sector	Lead Agency
Information and communications	Commerce
Banking and finance	Treasury
Water supply	Environmental Protection Agency
Aviation, highways, mass transit, pipelines, rail, waterborne commerce	Transportation
Emergency law enforcement services	Justice/FBI
Emergency fire service, continuity of government services	Federal Emergency Management Agency
Public health services	Health and Human Services
Electrical power, oil and gas production and storage	Energy
Federal government	General Services Administration

Sector officials from each of the lead agencies work with the national coordinator for security, infrastructure protection, and counterterrorism on the Critical Infrastructure Coordinating Group (CICG), an interagency committee charged with analyzing CIP policy and making recommendations to a cabinet-level principals committee.[5] Federal government functions without a clear private sector analog are assigned to special functional coordinators. These are shown in Table A.2.

---

[4] *Defending America's Cyberspace,* p. 23.

[5] *Defending America's Cyberspace,* p. 23. This structure changed with the new Administration in 2001. This interagency committee was absorbed into a broader policy coordination panel.

able

CP ecial unction gencies

Special Function Coordinators	
State Department	Foreign affairs
Defense	National defense
Central Intelligence Agency	Foreign intelligence
Justice/FBI	Law enforcement and internal security
Office of Science and Technology Policy	Research and development

Each of these entities and functional responsibilities bears on the appropriate resource allocation for critical infrastructure R&D. As indicated, OSTP has special responsibilities for coordinating government-wide research and development activities on CIP. This mandate translates into a critical role in evaluating the significance of Y2K for future R&D decisions.

Direct Y2K preparatory activities that created new capabilities in any of the infrastructure areas where lead agencies are active can be expected to have some bearing on U.S. capabilities for carrying out *functional activities* in critical infrastructure protection. Indirect activities—principally those carried out in the private sector—must also have affected CIP capabilities, if only because most critical infrastructures in the U.S. are privately owned and operated.[6] This translates into a considerable increase in the complexity of the CIP context post-Y2K. Where assessments of private sector CIP preparedness prior to the Y2K rollover were generally quite pessimistic, it is possible that infrastructure remediation efforts have lessened critical infrastructure vulnerability to deliberate (or inadvertent) disruptions. The migration toward newer information systems may have eradicated older system flaws. Newer infrastructure systems may, of course, possess their own as yet unappreciated vulnerabilities. In fact, some analysts have already raised the issue of increased network and computer system homogeneity (as Windows 9.x and Windows 2000 derivatives replace UNIX systems, for example) as a potential weakness in infrastructure protection.

The large financial investments (billions of U.S. dollars) of the private sector in remediation and system upgrades also suggest that a pre-Y2K assessment of the areas most in need of governmental CIP R&D support might need to be updated. This appendix does not claim to undertake such a large-scale reassessment, but rather continues the process of infrastructure protection policy development first exemplified by the *National Plan for Information Systems Protection*, version 1.0, *An Invitation to Dialogue*, and deepened by successor documents.

---

[6] The Report of the President's Commission on Critical Infrastructure Protection, *Critical Foundations: Protecting America's Infrastructures*, October 1997, Chapter Three.

Definitions

Definitions of systemic challenges are necessarily antecedent to discussions of the requisite R&D focuses required to meet them. Defining critical infrastructure vulnerabilities independently involves an examination of the character of networks, their vulnerability to deliberate or inadvertent disruption, and the degree to which remedial measures for countering weaknesses introduce potential new compromises into a global security model.[7] The term *challenges* is used here instead of *threats* because of the truism that, from the standpoint of a network's service delivery function, anything that interferes with critical operations serves to undermine its raison d'être.[8] From this perspective, two types of threats can be described: (1) threats from actors and/or entities targeting an infrastructure to achieve some political, criminal, or social objective; and (2) the more operational threat that *represents the means through which actors seek to achieve their disruptive objectives*. Research and development policy is appropriately aimed at the technical systems that stand between the disruptive intentions of threatening actors and their ultimate objectives. This narrowed focus of attention means that broader critical infrastructure protection issues are outside the scope of our attention, *except* to the extent that they inform assessments of the types of technical threats most likely to be exploited by potential adversaries, *and* to the extent that private sector protective investments are seen as inadequate for the protection of national security interests in a particular infrastructure context.

Two Conceptual Frameworks for Understanding Y2K and CIP Risks

Two conceptual frameworks—attack trees and statistical approaches—are outlined below which define a spectrum of CIP/risk management and response approaches. These frameworks are broadly representative of the slowly emerging literature on CIP responses.

Attack Trees as a CIP Analysis Framework

Attack trees are a version of a "top-down" logic tree framework for analyzing critical infrastructure protection problems. By examining the functionality of targeted infrastructures, defining a spectrum of alternative disruption targets, and then decomposing these elements into components framed against the requirements for restoring normal system operations, this approach allows for more comprehensive risk assessment and vulnerability analyses. One of the most articulate proponents of this approach is Bruce Schneier, chief technology officer and founder of Counterpane Security, a cryptographic and information security firm. Schneier is a well-known cryptographer and critic of infrastructure and computer security

---

[7] Rebecca Gurley Bace, *Intrusion Detection* (Indianapolis, IN: Macmillan, 2000), p. 32.

[8] Similarities between management challenges in Y2K and CIP further support this insight. The U.S. General Accounting Office concluded that there was broad complementarity between strategic responses in Y2K remediation and those required to secure critical infrastructures. See GAO, *Year 2000 Computing Challenge: Lessons Can Be Applied to Other Management Challenges* (GAO/AIMD-00-290, September 2000), especially the discussion of communications issues and improvements in information sharing. See pp. 18–21.

preparedness.[9] His approach—outlined in a paper entitled "Attack Trees"[10]—focuses on the potential targets of entities seeking to disrupt critical systems.

As Figure A.1 indicates, physical analogies can be used to introduce the logical issues involved in decomposing a system attack problem into its component parts. Schneier discusses the steps involved in planning an assault on a safe, relative to the level of difficulty and methods available for achieving the objective. At the fourth level of the attack tree, Schneier inserts values for the feasibility of executing the various options: threaten, blackmail, eavesdrop, or bribe (omitted on the graphic for clarity). In the context examined, the least costly (in resources or risk of discovery) way of gaining access to the safe combination is to eavesdrop on the conversation of someone who knows it. Additionally, getting someone to state the combination in an overheard conversation would also work.

RAND MR1259-A.1

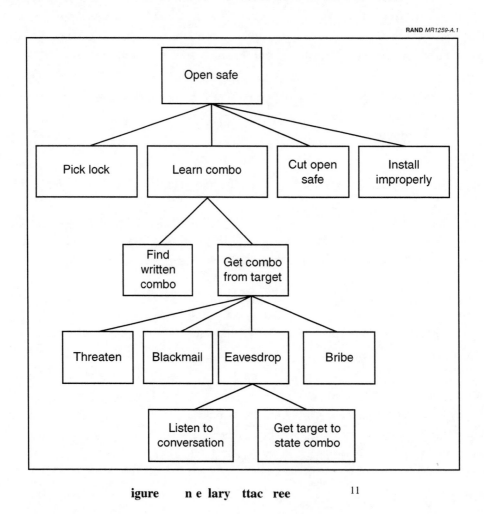

igure   n e lary ttac ree [11]

---

[9] Schneier is the author of the Twofish encryption algorithm, one of the finalists in NIST's competition to replace DES with an advanced digital encryption standard (ADES).

[10] Bruce Schneier, "Attack Trees," *Dr. Dobbs Journal*, December 1999 (http://www.ddj.com/articles/1999/9912/9912a/9912a.htm).

[11] Bruce Schneier, *Secrets and Lies: Digital Security in a Networked World* (New York: John Wiley, 2000), p. 319.

This example shows the utility of breaking up the problem—in this case, opening a safe—into manageable subtasks, each of which can be defined in terms of its overall criticality to achieving the objective, and potential risk due to the potential for discovery or mitigation (of the particular vulnerability). In critical infrastructure protection, systems and installations can also be described as security targets, where the objective of an attacker is either to disrupt system functions, to compromise the data within a system, or to gain control of that system to achieve some other objective. Put most directly:

> Any security target (infrastructure system or system complex comprising a set of linked subsystems) can be divided into a number of discrete subsystems that scale into an overall systems architecture.

Each of these defined subsystems possesses vulnerabilities with respect to the compromise of an overall security model or models protecting the integrity of the infrastructure involved. Relationships between subsystem vulnerabilities and overall security target robustness (understood as resistance to compromise) vary in value and may be both additive and/or complex-adaptive in nature. Finally, in a defined universe of security targets and subsystems, discrete sets of vulnerabilities can be discovered through an exploration of system features, systematic "red-team" audits of security preparations, and engineering examinations of software for flaws or exploitable errors.[12] The two most important features of discovered vulnerabilities are (1) the feasibility or likelihood of their exploitation, and (2) the overall criticality of a particular vulnerability for the security target/infrastructure as a whole.

For the first, vulnerability exposure utilization is either possible or impossible. If possible, then a probability of exploitation can be calculated, given appropriate data sources and testing methodologies. If impossible in the time horizon over which risk assessment is concerned, the vulnerability exposure can still be ranked for analysis against longer-term trajectories of the security target's technical evolution.[13] A vulnerability index, basically the risk of an exposed security target subsystem being compromised multiplied by the value (or criticality) of that subsystem to overall system integrity, may be calculated for any and all nodes making up a security target. Such calculations provide an initial numerical basis for assessing the risk exposure of infrastructures to *known security vulnerabilities*. Continuous audit activities allow for the systematic revisiting of node-level security conditions in order to revalidate the risk exposure of subsystems against a constantly evolving threat picture. Because infrastructures are dynamic systems that undergo continuous technical and operational change, however, static analyses based on fixed risk and vulnerability indices are unlikely to provide an up-to-date picture of critical infrastructure vulnerability. Instead, an awareness of subsidiary sources of vulnerability exposure is required. Process questions, focusing on the relationship of vulnerabilities to one another, and to the integrity of interdependent systems, must be examined in order for a more comprehensive picture of infrastructure vulnerability and risk to be created.

---

[12] Post hoc audits of deployed systems would seem to be fundamental to any approach at continuous validation of system or network integrity.

[13] The idea here is that a vulnerability that seems implausible in the short run may rise in importance due to technical and operational changes in a particular infrastructure system or in interdependent systems. Repeated audit and assessment of the importance of such system "features" is necessary for a high-confidence risk assessment of critical infrastructures to be constructed.

Attack Tree Structure and Process Issues

Attack trees allow for the decomposition of critical infrastructure vulnerability into smaller, more conceptually manageable portions. The logic of the approach stems from the use of probabilities and indices to indicate the relative robustness of particular parts of a system, together with the imputation of values relative to the individual and collective resource effort required to protect portions of an infrastructure designated as critical to core system functionality. More complex infrastructures, especially those utilizing networked computer-to-computer communications and distributed processing, may also be prone to less predictable sources of vulnerability and disruption. The next section outlines some potential issues that arise from this situation.

Attack Trees and Complex Adaptive Phenomena

Attack trees are complex and adaptive to the extent that programming or architecture errors at independently situated nodes propagate forward, backward, and between node levels with unpredictable strength and duration (see Figure A.2 below). Arbitrary node levels are defined according to classes dividing an infrastructure into subsidiary systems.[14] Each of these systems can be understood as comprising a number of components, together with a set of physical and logical relationships linking them together.[15] Relationships within node levels can be understood as representing common issue categories for a particular risk assessment or management exercise. Nodes related by level have discrete and architecturally well-understood relationships with neighbors and have relative independence from nodes in other levels. While, logically, a security target could perhaps be differentiated into an almost infinite number of levels, in actuality, the planning processes used in risk assessments are finite, thus converging on some optimal number of node levels, N, as defined in Figure A.2.

Each branch in the attack tree can be decomposed into subsidiary paths, with each one carrying a finite probability of both exploitation and independent (random or system-specific) disruption. In the earlier discussion, these two features were described in terms of two indices: a *vulnerability index* (v_i), representing the seriousness of a vulnerability for overall system integrity, and an *exploitation likelihood index* (l_i), determined by the classes of actors with the capability to utilize a vulnerability disrupt infrastructure functionality.[16] Assessments of actor capability necessarily emerge from an analysis of the history of a given group or individual in attack of similar systems, their level of technical expertise, and information linking them to particular threats or objectives proximate to a CIP incident.

---

[14] Clearly, these node levels may differ among and between infrastructure systems. More generally, however, it is assumed that comparable computing and networking technologies are being deployed throughout the economy. Multiple and interdependent systems are responsible for delivering infrastructure services to the public. Interdependencies among and between infrastructures thus produce potentially complex and difficult-to-predict disruption and failure possibilities.

[15] Note that computer systems have logical structures that may be more important than physical interconnections of components with respect to issues of fault tolerance and reliability.

[16] Trends in network attack tool development seem to point in the direction of "rootkits"—multipurpose weapons with increasingly point-and-click functionality. This change has dramatically reduced the skill level required for attackers to manifest serious disruptive capabilities. For a good summary of these trends, see Stephen Northcutt and Judy Novak, *Network Intrusion Detection: An Analyst's Handbook*, Second Edition (Indianapolis, IN: New Riders, 2000), pp. 217–240 and pp. 241–254.

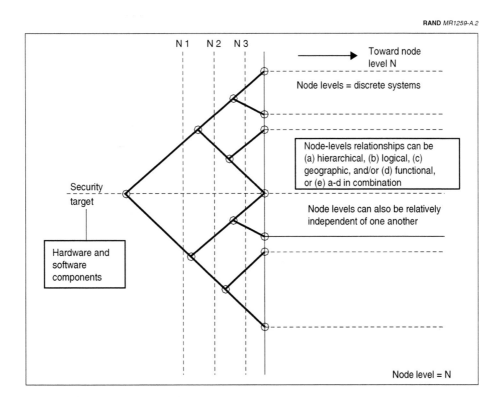

igure   o e-Le el Deco osition of a ecurity arget

Relationships between node levels add a layer of complexity to this picture, as nonprobabilistic factors come into play through the interactive uncertainties characteristic of different points in the attack tree. Logically, the direction of disruptive importance is left for serious infrastructure disruptive errors, and right for less-disruptive errors mitigated by redundancy and fault tolerance in an infrastructure's substructure.

How do different nodes relate to one another in the error or fault propagation issue? And, are different error conditions mutually reinforcing, leading to a multiplication effect if they are coincident, or do errors cancel each other out, indicative of deeper fault tolerance in a system?[17]

Calculations of infrastructure protection adequacy and the risk management rules and standards appropriate for a particular infrastructure are thus unlikely to emerge from any self-contained technical exploration of system vulnerabilities. Correspondingly, such determinations require an overall security policy containing standards reflecting the particular risk acceptance characteristics of a specific infrastructure domain (i.e., the air transportation system, the public switched network, the oil and gas distribution and storage system).

---

[17] Schneier, *Secrets and Lies*, pp. 158–159.

42

It is also possible that linked security targets—either within single infrastructures or through interdependencies—could manifest single points of failure due to the inadequate provision of redundancy or fault tolerance in deployed systems.[18] Analysis suggests that single-point failures fall into at least two separate categories. One kind of single-point failure would derive from an inappropriate concentration of critical functionality into a system with inadequate backup capacity or planning. Such a situation could arise through poor planning, or due to decentralized decisions regarding infrastructure components, technology deployments, and planning. A second form of single-point failure could arise from a complex systems effect, where a given node level, or trans-node-level relationship, creates effects that propagate in ways that produce a catastrophic failure of an infrastructure security target (see Figure A.3). Such an occurrence may go almost completely undetected in the absence of thorough modeling of infrastructure interdependencies. It is possible, however, that those genuinely complex adaptive phenomena may represent emergent properties in infrastructure networks. As such, their appearance may defy traditional modeling, revealing instead the more ephemeral—or less accessible—dynamics of complex adaptive phenomena.

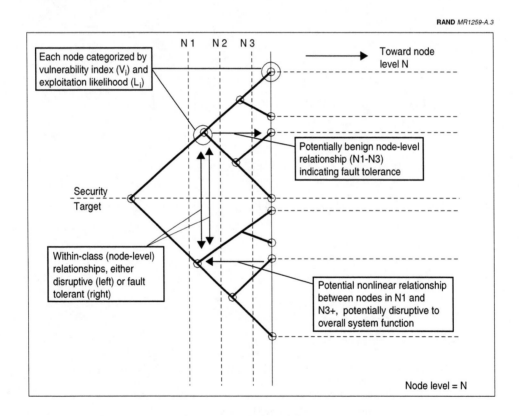

igure   Co le o e Deco osition a

---

[18] Note that Arthur Money, Assistant Secretary of Defense for Command, Control, Communications and Intelligence, has identified the proliferation of single-point failure nodes in infrastructures of importance to the Department of Defense's logistics and power projection functions.

Applying this approach from an individual system or facility to a complex of communications and computing systems is a matter of thoroughly documenting links between infrastructure subsystems—to establish a node-level decomposition of a security target—cataloging network traffic patterns, security policies, and different independent operating entities.[19] Once this information is collected, a structured representation of infrastructure linkages can be created. The listing of infrastructure features can be translated into a "logic tree" process comprising the iterative presentation of infrastructures from the standpoint of potential disruptive goals defined by a spectrum of hypothetical attackers.[20]

The infrastructure attack problem may be further decomposed into extremely detailed and complex descriptions of system/subsystem interaction. Understanding the links between disruptive events at the various levels of the logic tree is critical to calculating risk exposures in infrastructure protection. Different nodes on the tree can be assigned numerical probabilities (in terms of likelihood of inclusion in known exploits) and cost/risk factors, allowing for risk assessments to focus on those system features most likely to make an infrastructure vulnerable.

Recent analysis has corroborated the utility of a node-level decomposition of an information infrastructure. Reuven Cohen et al. used percolation theory—an approach based in mathematical physics—to discuss the stability of boundaryless networks in the face of randomized node disruption or destruction. The authors were able to establish the broad stability of large networks—explicitly, the internet—under conditions where over 90 percent of interconnected nodes were off-line. At the same time, however, they noted that the circumstances underlying this stability condition ensure continued connectivity—whether that connectivity is sufficient to ensure/allow critical functionality is a separate question. This issue, the crux of critical infrastructure protection, depends on the features of node-level relationships and the characteristics of the nodes themselves.[21]

Once a structured presentation of infrastructure protection dilemmas is achieved, this can be used to gauge the appropriate R&D prioritization for improving the protection of at-risk systems and infrastructures. An assumption is made at the outset that privately owned infrastructures would change over time consistent with industry and owner-operator perceptions of risk, threats to business continuity, and the regulatory environment. Where this self-interested risk assessment exceeds or matches national security-derived CIP efforts, clear synergies are possible between public and private sector research on critical infrastructure vulnerabilities.

If private sector risk assessments diverge significantly from governmental perspectives, then a shortfall in CIP resource allocation and R&D planning may occur. There are two parts to this potential problem: (1) short-run resources aimed at rectifying known vulnerabilities in deployed systems, and (2) longer-term

---

[19] Networks and network protocols are designed with a number of features, two of which are structure and abstraction. Network protocols, such as TCP/IP and X.25, describe software and hardware interaction according to conceptual layers deriving from the archetypal OSI model. Radia Perlman provides a good examination of this analytical position in *Interconnections Second Edition: Bridges, Routers, Switches, and Internetworking Protocols* (Reading, MA: Addison Wesley, 2000).

[20] David Mussington, "Throwing the Switch in Cyberspace," *Jane's Intelligence Review*, July 1996, pp. 331–334.

[21] Reuven Cohen, Keren Erez, Daniel ben-Avraham, and Shlomo Havlin, "Resilience of the Internet to Random Breakdowns," *Physical Review Letters*, Volume 85, Number 21 (20 November 2000), pp. 4626–4628.

developmental vulnerabilities deriving from planned or extant infrastructure upgrades, under-appreciated network vulnerabilities, undocumented system access modes, or novel attack methods developed by hackers.[22]

The potential for longer-term underinvestment is both quantitative and qualitative in nature. The infrastructurewide R&D resource allocation is the main issue for OSTP and its oversight function on federal CIP R&D expenditures. An attack tree perspective on an infrastructure CIP R&D agenda would make evident specific technical shortfalls in research attention, comparing, for example, private sector risk assessments with federal CIP R&D plans and programs on an iterative basis (through outreach to private sector infrastructures)—facilitated by the information-sharing and analysis centers (ISACs) established under PDD 63—and through focused vulnerability assessments of "high-leverage" parts of revealed attack trees.

Statistical Approaches

Statistical approaches for characterizing critical infrastructures begin by analyzing the reliability and known failure modes of network components, aggregating these connected subsystems into increasingly complex infrastructures, and then reaching conclusions regarding overall vulnerability and risk exposure.[23] Novel failure modes and newly discovered system vulnerabilities modify prior infrastructure assessment baselines, with technical and operational changes in infrastructure characteristics driving an iterative process of infrastructure evaluation.[24]

A critical assumption in statistical approaches is that linear, additive relationships exist between the security vulnerabilities of infrastructure components at the micro level and entire systems of interconnected computing and communications facilities (see Figure A.4).[25] Risk assessment frameworks based on this assumption evaluate infrastructure vulnerability against historical data on system behavior. Well-understood systems behave in a predictable fashion, presenting analysts with models of clear means/ends relationships that underlie system disruptions or breakdowns.[26] Infrastructures under rapid technical and operational changes are more difficult to model, creating the potential for significant divergences between predicted and actual behavior.[27] The virtuosity of adversaries seeking to penetrate apparently secure networked infrastructures also lessens theoretically achievable security levels. Known

---

[22] Statement for the record of Louis J. Freeh, Director, Federal Bureau of Investigation, on cybercrime, before the Senate Committee on Appropriations.

[23] Subcommittee for the Departments of Commerce, Justice, State, the Judiciary, and related agencies, February 16, 2000, p. 4.

[24] An example of this type of framework is the Operational Critical Threat, Asset and Vulnerability Evaluation (OCTAVE) framework developed at the Software Engineering Institute (SEI); see Christopher J. Alberts et al., Technical Report CMU/SEI-99-TR-017, June 1999.

[25] A critical assumption is that the stability and security characteristics of systems are scalable as they expand. The veracity of this position directly relates to the architectures of a particular system or facility.

[26] For the seminal discussion of this situation, see Charles Perrow, *Normal Accidents: Living with High Risk Technologies* (New York: Basic Books, 1984).

[27] See Roger Molander et al., *Strategic Information Warfare Rising* (Santa Monica, CA: RAND, MR-964-OSD, 1998), pp. 17–22 and pp. 39–42, for an analysis of different hedging strategies.

RAND *MR1259-A.4*

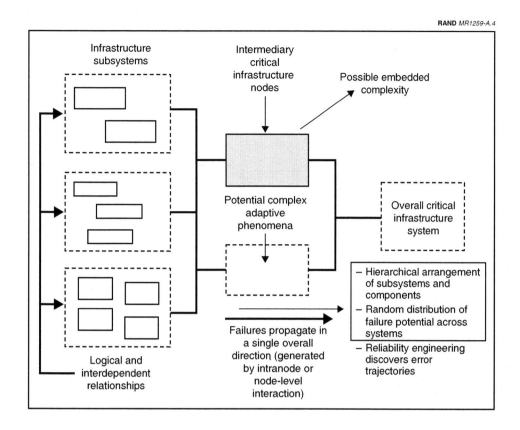

igure   Linear o e Deco osition a

but nonpublic operating system and network features present unauthorized actors with means of accessing networks.[28] Correspondingly, infrastructure operators face an uncertain environment within which the risk of network compromise interacts with undocumented network characteristics in unpredictable ways.[29]

A number of hypothetical relationships between undocumented system features and the assessed risk of infrastructure vulnerabilities can be conceptualized. One approach argues for a strong positive relationship, suggesting that closely held information on system features (proprietary APIs, undocumented software calls, etc.) and secrecy regarding successfully exploited system vulnerabilities may correlate with a heightened risk to critical infrastructures.[30]

---

[28] The exploitation of well-known flaws in network software by hackers is frequently linked to denial-of-service attacks and other network intrusion cases.

[29] See Molander et al. (1998), appendix on new frameworks, pp. 67–71.

[30] It is possible that open-source software design and peer review disciplines may offer a significant positive contribution to iterative error detection and system design processes. For an explication of this concept, see Eric Raymond, *The Cathedral and the Bazaar*, as excerpted on the web, http://www.firstmonday.dk/issues/issue3_3/raymond/.

A second approach presents a contrary perspective on the relationship between infrastructure risk and undocumented network features. Under this model, the risk of system compromise declines with the growth of undocumented network characteristics. Undocumented features are often associated with closed or proprietary software. A third possibility is that neither approach accurately (and independently) models infrastructures *in transition*, and that emergent properties account for the real distribution of critical infrastructure risks.

Even well-understood infrastructure systems confront the problem of emergent features in operations that went undetected during testing.[31] While not necessarily complex in nature, these phenomena may be almost completely random in distribution. Determining the frequency of such flaws in a deployed system or infrastructure requires a modeling approach that addresses both components and system architectures.[32] The uncertainties involved in validating technical systems as without serious flaws make this a significant—but still manageable—enterprise. Interconnections between simple and complex systems, however, may limit any validity assessments to broad statements of quality and likelihood.

Whichever characterization of infrastructure vulnerabilities is accepted, the task for planners seeking to hedge against the inherently uncertain critical infrastructure vulnerabilities is stark and difficult. Simulations of complex infrastructure systems may be a means for discovering interdependencies correlated with potential threats to system integrity. Two types of modeling suggest themselves: first, engineering studies on the reliability and stability of infrastructure systems; and second, research on the economic criticality of key systems to analyze the potential economic losses flowing from infrastructure disruptions. The latter area of research would help to establish a data set for comparisons of different security architectures relative to indices of tolerable risk.[33] Increasingly accurate simulations of infrastructure operation and interdependencies may substitute for real-world testing and research on vulnerabilities. Modeling of this type may also streamline R&D priority setting as a potential adjunct to public/private collaborative work on CIP standards and risk assessment methodologies.[34]

This discussion of baseline approaches to CIP is designed to show two of the different perspectives that can orient research and development priorities. These largely theoretical meta-approaches become concrete in the R&D definitions and priorities substantively applied by the U.S. government since PDD 63 was promulgated in 1998. The influence of the Department of Defense in the critical infrastructure protection policy area is significant. This influence derives from the increasing dependence of DoD on privately owned infrastructures, but also from the Defense Department's experience in targeting

---

[31] The usage of the term *emergent* here borrows from that of Bruce Schneier in *Secrets and Lies*, where he targets emergent flaws as sources of system insecurity.

[32] The node-level analysis framework introduced earlier in this appendix is an attempt to outline the minima of just such an approach.

[33] These indices would likely be generated by an assessment of the implications of particular risks for overall system integrity and service delivery. The economic value of system downtime and the real-world implications of losses in safety and security could be discovered through policy development and iterative analysis.

[34] For an analysis of infrastructure vulnerability that is suggestive of this type of approach, see Robert H. Anderson et al., *Securing the U.S. Defense Information Infrastructure: A Proposed Approach* (Santa Monica, CA: RAND, MR-993-OSD/NSA/DARPA, 1999).

investment dollars in R&D to create future-oriented capabilities calculated to meet established functional requirements. DoD definitions of R&D are thus an important input into the arena where CIP research priorities are determined.

Defining Research and Development for National Security

Research and development planning requires that decisions be made on where particular expenditures and program activities should be allocated. This allocation is a function of categorizing programs into at least two sets: (1) basic research, and (2) applied research leading to fielded technologies. This broad typology is the starting point for much more detailed work on the spectrum of activities between "pure" basic research and "pure" applied technology developments. The discussion below characterizes the divergent means through which the civil and defense research communities have often defined their activities and allocative choices.

Department of Defense Definitions

DoD uses a seven-point categorization for its research and development activities. The categories are:

6.1   Basic Research

6.2   Applied Research

6.3   Advanced Technology Development

6.4   Demonstration and Validation

6.5   Engineering and Manufacturing Development

6.6   RDT&E Management Support

6.7   Operational System Development

Residual categories of developmental test and evaluation and operational test and evaluation are also used.[35]

These R&D categories are prone to imprecision. As one group of analysts observes, programs are often labeled by DoD component organizations as 6.1 or 6.2 in nature, while research programs that deliver applications to the field (typically 6.3 or 6.4) might be labeled 6.1 or 6.2 if they were undertaken independently from a clearly articulated statement of requirements.[36]

---

[35] Donna Fossum et al., *Discovery and Innovation: Federal Research and Development Activities in Fifty States, the District of Columbia, and Puerto Rico* (Santa Monica, CA: RAND, MR-1194, 2000), Appendix B.

[36] John A. Alic et al., *Beyond Spinoff: Military and Commercial Technologies in a Changing World* (Cambridge, MA; Harvard University Press, 1992), p. 107.

During the Cold War, "spinoff" arguments were widely used to assert clear and unambiguous links between defense-supported research and development and the growth of civilian applications. As the Cold War recedes from view, however, these arguments are less and less salient, especially as commercial research and development expenditures came to dominate national totals.[37] It is still likely, however, that DoD R&D choices influence the qualitative balance of activities in the private sector research portfolio, if only due to the significance of federal government support for academic research through DARPA and other agencies.[38]

Civil Sector Research and Development Definitions

The National Science Foundation's categorization of research and development resembles the initially described spectrum from basic to applied research. As the definitions read:

> Basic research is defined as research directed to ards increases in no ledge ... ithout specific application to ard processes or products in mind. Applied research is defined as no ledge or understanding for determining the means by hich a recogni ed and specific need may be met, and development is the systematic use of the no ledge or understanding gained from research directed to ards the production of useful materials, devices, systems, or methods, including design and development of prototypes and processes.[39]

Using this definition of research and development activities, it is clear that the design of products is not commonly viewed as R&D. Rather, the spread of marketing to applied technological processes and products may become synchronized with classically defined R&D activities as the private sector comes to dominate the agenda of science and engineering in computing and communications technologies. In such an environment, it is difficult to rationalize traditional views of public sector R&D as the leading edge of planning and exploration in advanced technologies. Instead, private sector imperatives will structure the trajectory of change in infrastructures, in terms of both risk and vulnerability assessments associated with individual computer and communications systems *and* longer-term contingency plans aimed at increasing the service delivery capabilities of existing and future networks.

Critical Infrastructure Protection and "Derived" Research and Development Concepts

CIP analysis frameworks and traditional ways of approaching R&D may not be entirely consistent with one another. It is also true, however, that "top-down" (government-led) or "bottom-up" (private sector-initiated) approaches to CIP may need to be combined in order to fully take account of the private sector-biased CIP development and policy environment. Proposals for joint public/private information sharing and infrastructure protection activities would logically require a parallel research and development strategy, emphasizing *joint* priority setting in longer-term CIP R&D planning, and an in-depth analysis of

---

[37] Ibid., p. 110.

[38] Ibid., p. 111

[39] Ibid., p. 106.

the extent to which private infrastructure protection actions and priorities overlap with (or fail to include) governmental CIP interests and objectives. Evaluation criteria for critical infrastructure protection R&D policies flow from more general CIP issues, as research and development programs largely derive from these broader priority agendas. It remains the case, however, that R&D priorities determined in the absence of an adjudication of the appropriate public/private CIP activity set confront the very real prospect of substantive irrelevance.

National Plan Critical Infrastructure R&D Priorities

The President's Commission on Critical Infrastructure Protection (PCCIP) created a template for the initial research and development agenda on CIP. The context for critical infrastructure R&D planning was the nine focus areas identifying critical functions and services delivered over computing and communications networks. These nine categories were later consolidated into six core areas:

1. Banking and finance

2. Information and communications

3. Energy

4. Transportation

5. Vital human services

6. Interdependencies

The national plan for information systems protection released in January of 2000 proposes 10 programs designed to advance critical infrastructure protection objectives. These are:

1. Identify critical infrastructure assets and shared interdependencies and address vulnerabilities

2. Detect attacks and unauthorized intrusions

3. Develop robust intelligence and law enforcement capabilities to protect critical information systems, consistent with the law

4. Share attack warnings and information in a timely manner

5. Create capabilities for response, reconstitution, and recovery

6. Enhance research and development in support of programs 1–5

7. Train and employ adequate numbers of information security specialists

8. Outreach to make Americans aware of the need for improved cyber-security

9. Adopt legislation and appropriations in support of programs 1–8

10. In every step and component of the plan, ensure the full protection of American citizens' civil liberties, their rights to privacy, and their rights to the protection of proprietary data.

Program 6 includes a number of initiatives described in Appendix C of the national plan document. In the context of the foregoing discussion of possible divergences between public and private sector R&D priorities based on varying estimations of risk, the national plan seeks to foster progress toward a coherent national planning agenda meeting the requirements of both communities. In order to meet the deadlines set in the May 1998 Presidential Decision Directive (PDD 63) and within the national plan, the R&D agenda must

> [Achieve] intrusion detection systems that ideally have high detection rates and low false alarm rates. It will also require systems that can isolate problem portions of infrastructures and either "heal" them quickly or rapidly bring substitute capability online, all while protecting the rest of the infrastructures from harm. It will not be enough to meet the PDD 63 deadlines of 2001 and 2003.

Evolving technologies that provide new avenues for critical infrastructure disruption will necessitate a continuing R&D program to maintain our critical infrastructures in a robust condition.

The critical infrastructure protection interagency working group thus drafted—under the Critical Infrastructure Coordination Group's (CICG) guidance—an R&D agenda designed to capture the predictable future of infrastructures within knowable bounds of development.

National Plan Research Objectives

The national plan articulates a lengthy agenda of 71 different initiatives across the six infrastructure areas identified. Overarching themes or objectives designed to focus activities in each of the named sectors include:

> [Fostering] an awareness of the state of new technological developments as they become embedded in infrastructures and the new avenues they present for hostile and non-hostile disruption of these architectures;

> [Creating] an ability to produce an affordable menu of R&D programs in critical infrastructure protection in time to be useful to those who make resource allocation and infrastructure protection planning decisions in government and the private sector;

> [Fostering] a functioning, effective two-way interaction with the private sector, academia, and other countries so that R&D overlap is minimized and programs are pursued that best meet the needs of the private sector and government; and

[Developing] an innovative management structure that is sufficiently flexible and responsive to a rapidly changing infrastructure environment in terms of [both] technology and threats.[40]

The R&D/Policy Interface

The R&D agenda for each sector is lengthy and is sampled here for illustrative purposes only. The information and communications and energy infrastructures are viewed by many observers as the most fundamental CIP concerns. R&D priorities in these infrastructures are listed below:

Information and communications

Modeling and simulation tools

Vulnerability detection, assessment, and analysis

Response, recovery, and reconstitution

Reliability, survivability, and robustness

Risk management, performance tools, security testing, and metrics

Core research capabilities, benchmarking, and recommended practices

Security architectures

Assurance technologies

Intrusion and incident detection and warning

Energy

Vulnerability assessments

Critical consequence analysis

Development of real-time control mechanisms

Development of high-security SCADA systems

Development of efficient, adaptable encryption

Development of robust authentication and authorization

Sensor and warning technology

---

[40] *Defending America's Cyberspace*, Appendix C, p. 129.

Transmission and distribution systems in the electric power industry

> Emergency response and recovery procedures

> Evaluation of policy effects

> Directed energy technology countermeasures

> Analysis of scale and complexity

Online security assessments

> Dispersed generation

Decision support systems

> Evaluation of institutional barriers

> Threat assessment for risk management

The above lists demonstrate a high degree of overlap between R&D in each of the three major infrastructures. This is to be expected, as the interdependencies between the three spheres are high and increasingly complex. The national plan goes further and parallels its treatment of interdependencies by addressing them as a "sixth" infrastructure area for the purposes of R&D planning. The list of research topics under interdependencies seeks to capture the degree of linkage between different infrastructures—both in search of emergent properties of clustered infrastructures and as a means of closing undiscovered gaps in coverage:

Interdependencies

> Characterization of interdependencies

> Complexity theory

> Modeling and simulation

> Vulnerability studies

> Mitigation technologies

> Policy research

In addition to these separate, listed priorities in CIP research, the national plan identifies cross-cutting areas for near-term attention: intrusion detection and monitoring and automated infrastructure control systems. These require immediate treatment because of their criticality and (presumably) the likelihood of achieving important results. Accordingly, 31 of the 71 programs launched across each of the six designated focus areas are designed to address these two priorities.

Some Conclusions on R&D in Critical Infrastructure Protection

Critical infrastructure protection requires intensified research into the principal sources of vulnerability that impact economic, public safety, and national security values. The private sector is likely to lead in any infrastructurewide technology development efforts designed to increase levels of security. Owners and operators of critical infrastructures share both a fiduciary duty to shareholders and a public trust to their customers. These two incentives for providing continuity of service should increase the overall level of CIP preparedness in the future. Where situations arise that threaten to undermine national security, however, the federal government can be expected to act in defense of national goals and priorities. Among these priorities is the safety and security of critical infrastructures in the U.S. and in the countries where the U.S. has friends and interests.

Targeting U.S. government investments in CIP R&D must be done in a way that catalyzes private sector research without crowding out innovation. Mechanisms for achieving this goal range from subsidization of independent R&D (IR&D) activities through accelerated dissemination of government-developed technical information and intellectual property. Whichever means is chosen, the goal is to enhance the long-term safety and security of critical infrastructures, mitigating vulnerability to deliberate disruptions even as the systems and institutions making up the infrastructures change.

Y2K and CIP are related to each other through the linkages—both direct and indirect—between different infrastructure systems. Disruptive effects can propagate through interdependent infrastructures. These interdependencies can be well understood or not understood at all. Direct linkages in well-understood and linearly interdependent infrastructures can be expected to produce predictable results, even if only in retrospect (post mortems often revealing previously unknown causal linkages).

Statistical analyses of vulnerabilities at particular infrastructure nodes can be used to define valid risk/vulnerability distributions, potentially usable for calculating vulnerability profiles. Infrastructure systems with more logical and physical complexity—deriving from both automated sources and/or the harshness of their operating environments—may have less predictable vulnerability profiles. As node-level complexities emerge and the direction of fault propagation becomes more difficult to model, statistical analyses of system vulnerabilities become less useful. As a result, a complex adaptive systems framework may be a better formulation for describing complex information infrastructures in transition, especially as increasingly sophisticated control and sensor architectures are deployed. What does this mean for the alleged similarities between Y2K and CIP? First, it is possible that critical infrastructures are less vulnerable to software- and hardware-based flaws than was previously assumed. This would provide a partial explanation for the apparent overestimation of foreign Y2K infrastructure vulnerabilities. At the same time, such a conclusion would also serve as justification for remediation activities in those systems where computer-based sensor and/or control systems *were* deployed. Pronounced explanatory uncertainties would also make remediation expenditures fit into the category of prudential insurance. Diagnosis of *selective* Y2K remediation as prudential leads to a concern with the available database on activities and discoveries that were developed during the remediation process. Unfortunately, this record is spotty and mostly impressionistic, with assessments of the Y2K experience only rarely producing in-depth qualitative and quantitative overviews of the Y2K outcome. Unfortunately, it appears that few cross-infrastructure data retention efforts were launched prior to the Y2K rollover.[41]

---

[41] This means that potentially valuable data on infrastructure interdependencies may have been lost.

Appendix B
Workshop Materials

Part One Discussion Objectives

The Y2K rollover was anticipated as a potentially disruptive and dangerous period. Failures in critical infrastructures could have caused interruptions in vital services, imposed economic costs on society, and placed at risk national and international security. That none of these events came to pass does not remove the strategic significance of the infrastructures exposed to Y2K problems, or the problems of risk assessment that made the rollover period so uncertain.

The scenario vignettes presented below are designed to aid a structured examination of these issues in the light of the Y2K experience. The vignettes are counter-historical examples, based on actual forecasts created to guide government contingency planning for foreign Y2K eventualities. Though these events did not occur, they nonetheless represent a set of expectations and forecasts of possible Y2K situations and policy problems. The three vignettes are introduced below.

- Russian/Ukrainian/Polish natural gas crisis (involved infrastructures: oil and gas storage and distribution, electric power generation and distribution)

- Italian/Central Europe financial crisis (involved infrastructures: banking and financial services, information and communications)

- North American cyber/physical terrorism (infrastructures involved: electric power generation and distribution, transportation, information and communications)

Part One Instructions

In this section you are asked to answer a series of questions in the light of both your own Y2K remediation and contingency planning experience, but also in relation to the forecasts of potential Y2K disruptions described below. In this way it is hoped that prior thinking regarding credible potential Y2K disruptions can be closely considered in the light of actual "real-world" remediation and business continuity planning.

Three Counter-Historical Examples

Vignette #1: Russian/Ukrainian/Polish Natural Gas Crisis

Moscow, October 14 – The Russian minister of energy is informed that an end-to-end Y2K remediation test of the SCADA system for the Gazprom main gas line west of Moscow was a catastrophic failure. The test had induced a pumping substation malfunction, which caused a large explosion and fire.

Moscow, December 1 – The German ambassador in Moscow reports that based on a number of private conversations with Russian officials, he "and most knowledgeable Russians" have "absolutely no confidence that the Russian natural gas pipeline system is anywhere near Y2K compliant."

Russia and Ukraine, January 1, 0900 (local time) – The main pumping and pressure control station for the Gazprom main line outside Smolensk explodes. Just before the explosion, the senior Gazprom flow control manager in Moscow receives a frantic phone call from the on-site manager reporting the "catastrophic failure of a gas flow control valve." Nearly simultaneously, control failures occur along the Gazprom mainline that runs through Ukraine, with reports of explosions and fires at several pumping stations.

Moscow – The Gazprom natural gas pipeline failures that started on 1/1/00 unfortunately occur during the midst of one of the worst winter seasons on record in western Russia.

Czestochowa, Poland, January 2, 1600 (local time) – The Enzo Ltd. chemical plant suffers a series of catastrophic explosions and fires, sending a cloud of poisonous chlorine across the city. Early damage assessments report few fatalities but hundreds of serious casualties.

St. Petersburg, Russia, January 2, 1700 (local time) – Both nuclear power plants southeast of the city are shut down on an emergency basis. This results in a blackout of the St. Petersburg region. Internet reports indicate that the situation in St. Petersburg is "worrisome but there is no immediate indication of an outright nuclear accident." The shutdowns of the reactor control systems appear to have been prompted by the failure to prepare for the Y2K problem.

St. Petersburg, January 3, 1100 (local time) – The U.S. ambassador's chief economic officer warns him that an emergency shutdown of the two local reactors in St. Petersburg would cause "brownouts and blackouts throughout the region and also impact southern Finland."

Moscow, January 4 – Thousands of people in Moscow suffer from exposure due to inadequate heating. Local hospitals are overburdened. Brownouts and other electrical problems exacerbate this problem. It is unclear how long repairs will take, since some natural gas pumping and distribution stations have exploded, and fires continue to rage in places. (Some isolated distribution stations are snowed in and inaccessible, especially with relevant equipment.)

Poland, January 5 – The Russian Gazprom natural gas distribution system failure shuts down most natural gas flow into Poland, resulting in extensive heating outages in northern and eastern Poland, including the Warsaw and Gdansk areas. Widespread failures occur on the Polish electric power grid. The failures are attributed to control systems based on old Soviet computer mainframes, inexact clones of western designs from the 1970s–1980s, plus Soviet microprocessors that are also inexact clones of western designs. These systems are non-Y2K compliant. It is very difficult for anyone—from Russia, Poland, or western nations—to fix and remediate these systems, because of nonstandard hardware designs, poor to nonexistent software documentation, and the shortage of software experts in critical geographic locations. For these reasons, it is difficult to determine when these systems can be brought online—it could take weeks or months.

These electrical and natural gas system failures are causing the collapse of many public services such as hospitals, emergency response transportation, communications, and others. As a result, in major cities throughout Poland, older citizens are dying from the cold, sick people are dying in hospitals, food distribution is disrupted, and businesses are not operating.

Ukraine/Belarus, January 5 – Ukraine and Belarus are reporting widespread humanitarian emergencies throughout major portions of their countries. The electrical power failures are destroying medical supplies that require refrigeration, and many patients on life-support systems are dying. Backup generators at some key medical and emergency-response facilities were short of diesel fuel at the start of this calamity due to the harsh winter conditions during December, and backup generators failed throughout the region from two to five days after the initial 1/1/00 power failures.

Vignette #2: Italian/Central Europe Crisis

Rome, October 6 – Italian National Television airs a report claiming that the Italian banking system's Y2K remediation effort is "an absolute mess." Further, the report asserts that Y2K remediation software companies controlled by the Italian mafia may have compromised the data management systems of several major banks. The Italian stock market fell 15%, with several Italian bank stocks failing by more than 25% by the end of the trading day.

Milan, October 7 – After the Italian stock market fell by another 20%, the president of the European Central Bank announced that interest rates on the euro would be cut by another 0.5% (50 basis points). He denied that this move was prompted by the current economic situation.

Rome, October 9 – Italian police investigating an attempted break-in at the Italian Ministry of Finance discover that the thieves possessed sophisticated eavesdropping equipment and smart-card duplicates that were used to enter secure communications facilities in the basement of the building. During a subsequent interrogation, one of the thieves reveals that the Yugoslav government paid them for information on Italian government monetary policies and financial dealings. The police do not believe this story because several of the thieves possess known ties to a Russian transnational criminal organization (TCO).

Laufenberg, Switzerland, October 13 – Swiss federal police inform the FBI liaison team in Bern that unknown parties had attempted to break into the Laufenberg power generation and distribution complex by placing a series of trap doors in the main load-balancing software. The Swiss police emphasize that disruption of the Laufenberg facility could affect electric power grids throughout much of France, Bavaria, and Switzerland.

Rome, October 15 – The banking and financial crisis in Italy deepens due to rumors that the leading Italian banks are not prepared for Y2K.

Europe, October 25-26 – A major late fall storm produces severe icing conditions and results in widespread power outages in southern Germany, Switzerland, and the Czech Republic.

Switzerland, January 1, 0016 (local time) – The Laufenburg power distribution system in Switzerland suffers a series of interconnected failures, prompting the electric power grid to shed power in Bavaria and Alsace Lorraine. An attempt to balance the system throughout the German grid along the Rhine fails.

The Netherlands, January 1, 0020 (local time) – The Dutch Power Authority declares a "national emergency" and attempts to "islandize" the Dutch power grid from its European neighbors—leading to a brownout throughout Holland and related electric power failures in Luxembourg and Belgium.

Central Europe, January 1, 0200 (local time) – With snow and sleet falling at a record rate throughout the region, national weather forecasters in Switzerland, Germany, Austria, Slovenia, and northern Italy declare winter weather emergencies. A severe ice storm in central Italy downs power lines and causes grid power failures in Italy as far south as Florence.

Europe, January 4 – All major European stock exchanges fall sharply, with Italy experiencing the largest loss of 50%. During the day, the euro and the dollar oscillate wildly on the global currency markets. The value of the euro falls to 85¢ U.S., on the strength of rumors that the ECB Management Committee is unable to agree on an appropriate market intervention strategy.

Rome, January 4 – The Italian government nearly loses a vote of confidence. Later that evening, political commentators forecast that the government's days are numbered and anticipate that major Italian parties will campaign for a return of the lira.

Vignette #3: North American Cyber/Physical Terrorism

Mexico, November 22 – The Minister of the Interior informs the U.S. ambassador that the Mexican government has evidence that regional insurgent groups in Chiapas and Oaxaca are planning a military operation on or shortly after January 1st in anticipation of major Mexican Y2K problems that would "seriously discredit the government." His concerns are further amplified by private reports that "all is not well" with the Mexican electric power grids because of continued Y2K remediation problems.

Bern, December 20 – The director of the Swiss federal police announces the arrest of several members of "an apparent Christian Identity New Millennium cyberwarfare cell" that had undertaken "a systematic effort to penetrate the control systems of the electric power grids in Switzerland, France, and Germany." He privately informs the director of the FBI of evidence suggesting that a similar cell is operating in Canada and targeting the U.S. and Canadian electric power grids.

Atlanta, December 30 – CNN airs a "special report" citing evidence in the hands of U.S. and European law enforcement officials that Russian, Italian, Colombian, and Mexican organized crime groups are "successfully exploiting the eleventh-hour Y2K remediation panic of recent months." The report claims that organized crime penetrated the data management systems of a large number of small and medium-sized banks, brokerage firms, and selected businesses. This report is the latest in a series that CNN (like many other news outlets) is running on Y2K—almost all of them increasingly alarmist about the international Y2K situation, with some recent reports questioning previously optimistic assessments of U.S. Y2K readiness.

Jerusalem and Chicago, December 30 – U.S. and Israeli law enforcement authorities launch simultaneous raids on the offices of the Christian Identity New Millennium movement. The raids are prompted by tactical intelligence that the group was about to launch a terrorist bombing campaign to coincide with the millennium. Details regarding Christian Identity Group plans are sparse, but unnamed officials voice satisfaction that they succeeded in preventing potentially devastating attacks on government and religious sites in both the U.S. and Israel.

Princeton, New Jersey, January 1, 0010 (local time) – The North American Electric Reliability Council (NERC) receives numerous reports from systems operators throughout Massachusetts and Connecticut that central control stations are dealing with corrupt synchronous optical network (sonet) systems. The reports reveal that sonet message packet headers appear to be modified by an "unknown but very sophisticated intruder," leading to a "corruption of the distributed databases in the network."

Ontario and Quebec, January 1, 0012 (local time) – 55% of the electric power grid in Ontario goes off line. Within seconds, 40% of the Quebec hydro-electricity transmission network begins to shed power.

New York and Connecticut, January 1, 0015 (local time) – An extensive power failure blacks out much of the New York metropolitan area and western Connecticut. With most of Manhattan in the dark and massive crowds paralyzing the streets around Times Square, the mayor of New York City declares a citywide emergency.

Massachusetts and Connecticut, January 1, 0020 (local time) – The circuit breakers on a large number of electricity transmission substations in Massachusetts and Connecticut unexpectedly flip open. Attempts by central control stations in Massachusetts and Connecticut to close the circuit breakers are unsuccessful.

Boston, January 1, 0030 (local time) - Boston Edison reports that ten substations in the Boston region are not responding to messages sent to them through the sonet system. Later reports from repair crews indicate that "some mixture of damage caused by the ice storm and physical sabotage appeared to have caused major shorts and damage to substation transformers."

On the internet, January 1, 0035 (EST) – Major news sites on the World Wide Web are hacked by a group warning that reprisals for the "heavy handed and brutal" treatment of the Christian Identity Group are "at hand." The website hacks include quotes from the Old Testament, promising revenge against unbelievers and a "final judgment" against the "corrupt idolaters of the earth." The group also issues a "call to arms" to all "true believers insulted by the cruelty and ignorance of the U.S. and Israeli governments."

New York, January 1, 0130 (local time) – The flow control systems from the natural gas company supplying lower Manhattan and the Bronx inexplicably shut down the entire system for seven minutes, turning off the pilot lights in almost all multistory buildings in the region. Company representatives operating on emergency power immediately alert the media and police and fire authorities of the "critical need" to caution residential users not to attempt to relight their own pilot lights.

Chiapas and Oaxaca, January 1, 0400 (local time) – Armed insurgents attack Mexican police stations and army barracks in Chiapas and Oaxaca, producing light causalities. Two hours later, a coalition of Mexican insurgent groups announces via the Internet a "combined offensive to liberate Mexico." Mexican police and military authorities immediately dismiss these threats as "political theater" on Mexican television and radio.

Chicago, January 1, 0900 (local time) – A series of explosions rocks the Chicago Mercantile Exchange. The bombs partially collapse the front of the building and seriously damage a number of automobiles and neighboring buildings. An apparent breakdown in the 911 system serving the Chicago metropolitan region impedes the response of emergency services. As a result, fire and police vehicles do not arrive at the explosion site until 45 minutes after the explosions. Witnesses attempting to alert the 911 service experience busy signals or lose dial tones.

A CB radio operator in the area of the Mercantile Exchange finally alerts emergency services of the explosions. It is later revealed that the main computer network of the 911 system was penetrated by a hacker attack. The main switches for the 911 link to the public switched network were also physically damaged.

Los Angeles and San Diego, January 1 – Shipping traffic entering the ports of Los Angeles and San Diego is disrupted by an apparent Y2K-related corruption of key shipping management databases at the Customs Service. Schedules for inspections and records of ship manifests are also lost as Oracle databases at the Customs Service regional offices in San Diego and Los Angeles are corrupted by an apparent virus infection.

In an apparently unrelated incident, email service for the Customs Service is also interrupted by a severe SYN flood denial-of-service attack against a Los Angeles area internet service provider. Regular service is not restored for over two days. The Customs Service is unable to restore shipping control and inventory/manifest data from offsite secure backups.

Road traffic is also disrupted in proximity to both ports by breakdowns in the traffic management systems affecting local road networks. Traffic lights around both ports flash red or are stuck on red for most of the morning.

In addition, emergency services are disrupted by Y2K-related errors in the databases routing 911 phone calls. As a result, a major traffic accident at the main port entrance in San Diego is unattended by emergency services for several hours.

New England and eastern New York, January 2 – New York City and large parts of New England are without full electric power.

New England and eastern New York, January 3 – Boston, Hartford, and New York City continue to suffer brownouts. In New York, gas explosions and fires from attempts to light pilot lights are widespread.

Atlanta, January 3, 1700 (local time) – A Christian Identity representative in an interview with a CNN correspondent denies any connection with power failures in North America or the bombing in Chicago.

Washington, D.C., January 4, 1900 (local time) – The President requests an NSC meeting to discuss the deteriorating global situation stemming from the wide spectrum of Y2K failures and contemporaneous disruptive actions—with particular concern about the possible acts of terrorism in North America and the unsettled situations in Mexico.

Explaining the Y2K Outcome

The scenario vignettes presented above represent forecasts of events that did not occur. The particular reasons for the absence of any significant Y2K infrastructure disruptions are controversial. In the absence of data on the history of remediation efforts in different infrastructures, it is difficult to put together a coherent picture that adequately explains observed results. A number of candidate explanations for the phenomenon have been offered. Below is the list of hypotheses stated in the introduction, together with more focused statements of their possible meaning in the context of the scenarios:

1. The Y2K outcome was the result of effective remediation efforts carried out by a collaborative program involving the public and private sectors.

   - When unremediated Y2K problems surfaced at the time of the rollover, workarounds were readily implemented because everyone was at a very high state of alert (or because those problems that did emerge were not hard to fix).

2. The Y2K outcome was the result of independent private sector remediation and contingency planning efforts, with minimal involvement by governments.

- Eleventh-hour remediation efforts were successful because late remediators with significant dependencies were readily able to take advantage of the body of previous Y2K remediation work.

3. The Y2K outcome was the result of government-led efforts at energizing the private sector risk assessment and technology investments in a manner that protected vital critical infrastructures from date-related disruptions.

   - The motivation of malevolent actors to cause cyberspace disruptions was overestimated.

4. Y2K was never a systemic threat to critical infrastructures.

   - There was far less foreign infrastructure dependence on date-specific software and hardware than was projected by experts.

5. The cyber-dependence of critical infrastructures was overestimated, hence reducing the significance of Y2K-related network disruptions.

   - Needed remediation efforts were completed or well under way, and this was not recognized via existing sources of information.

6. The Y2K outcome is inadequately explained by any of the available models of critical infrastructure protection and infrastructure interdependencies. Therefore, any final judgments should be withheld.

   - Existing analytical frameworks were ill-suited to the problem of assessing infrastructure Y2K vulnerability.

Considering each of the scenario vignettes presented, please give your best explanation for why the events described did not occur.

Scenario Vignette #1: Russian/Ukrainian/Polish natural gas crisis

_____

_____

_____

_____

_____

Scenario Vignette #2: Italian/Central Europe crisis

_____

_____

_____

_____

_____

Scenario Vignette #3: North American cyber/physical terrorism

_____

_____

_____

_____

_____

Information-Sharing Issues

The sharing of information within infrastructures, across infrastructures, and between the private sector and government is one issue where critical infrastructure protection has exposed troubling impediments to progress. Many commentators suggest that the Y2K experience facilitated the creation of new or previously underutilized information-sharing channels for the dissemination of remediation data. Please address these issues in the light of the questions posed below.

1.   What new collaborative and information-sharing processes, mechanisms, or institutions did you observe (either within your infrastructure or across infrastructures) or utilize before, during, and subsequent to the Y2K rollover?

        _____a. Governmentally facilitated information-sharing and technology transfer processes

        _____b. Industry-level collaborative solution finding through "task forces" or information-sharing and analysis centers (ISACs)

        _____c. Interactive mechanisms involving business, government, and academia

        _____d. Other processes or responses

_____

_____

_____

_____

2.   What was your assessment of the information-sharing environment prior to the Y2K rollover?

      _____a.   Highly transparent, favoring exchanges of information in part prompted by the "Y2K safe haven" bill passed by Congress in 1999

      _____b.   Transparent within infrastructure sectors, with little cross-infrastructure learning or information exchange

      _____c.   Differentially transparent across infrastructures

      _____d.   Highly opaque. Information sharing was discouraged due to:

            _____ i.   Concerns with legal liability

            _____ii.   Regulatory concerns

            _____iii.   Underdeveloped information-sharing processes at the enterprise, infrastructure, or governmental/national levels

            _____iv.   No overall conclusion on this subject is possible

            _____v.   Other response

3.   What is your assessment of the information-sharing environment during the Y2K rollover?

      _____a.   Highly transparent, favoring exchanges of information

      _____b.   Transparent within infrastructure sectors, with little cross-infrastructure learning or information exchange

      _____c.   Differentially transparent across infrastructures

      _____d.   Highly opaque. Information sharing was discouraged due to:

            _____i.   Concerns with legal liability

            _____ii.   Regulatory concerns

            _____iii.   Underdeveloped information-sharing processes at the enterprise, infrastructure, or governmental/national levels _____iv.   No overall conclusion on this subject is possible

_____e. Other response

Organizational Issues

One area of analytical controversy is that of the relative value of different organizational models for responding to Y2K remediation *implementation* challenges. Where they exist, post mortems on Y2K remediation rarely focus on actual mechanics of organizing systematic assessment, remediation, and solution validation efforts. Instead they focus on particular programming techniques for addressing families of software errors. Please comment on your own experience of organizing Y2K remediation activities in your agency, enterprise, or company.

1.   How was the Y2K remediation process organized in your institution or company?

      _____ a   Single enterprisewide coordinator with division-level problem definition and remediation method selection with outsourced implementation of remediation measures and validation/audit tasks

      _____b.   Special division-level task forces led by senior executives with implementing personnel drawn from line business units rather than outsourced

2.   What infrastructure or sector-specific information resources or tools did your enterprise utilize or create in order to implement Y2K remediation?

      _____a.   Specialized industry-specific databases

      _____b.   Information processing tools and techniques for enterprisewide risk and vulnerability assessment

      _____c.   Standardized risk mitigation products or measures

      _____d.   Custom-designed or commissioned remediation mechanisms

      _____e.   Other items

_____

_____

_____

_____

Infrastructure Interdependencies

The scenario vignettes present examples of assumed infrastructure interdependencies, where failures in one set of systems cascade to others that may have been successfully remediated. In the absence of disruptive Y2K events, many observers question whether the level of interdependence among and between infrastructures is exaggerated. Relating the sequence of events and interdependencies discussed in the scenario vignettes to your own experience during the Y2K remediation process, please discuss any novel or underappreciated interdependencies that you became aware of due to your participation in Y2K remediation efforts.

1. Were cross-infrastructure interdependencies revealed during the remediation or solution validation phase of the Y2K rollover?

   _____a. Yes.

   _____b. No.

   If so, which infrastructure linkages were visible to you?

   _____i.   Information and communications/electric power

   _____ii.   Transportation/information and communications

   _____iii.   Oil and gas storage and distribution/information and communications

   _____iv.   Information and communications/vital human services

   _____v.   Other relationships

   _____

   _____

2. Drawing on the presentation of cross-infrastructure issues in the scenario vignettes and on your own experience, how would you characterize the importance of system vulnerabilities (i.e., control system anomalies, business process disruptions, service delivery interruptions) during the Y2K risk assessment process?

   _____a.   Mostly mission-critical

   _____b.   Serious, but correctable through readily available workarounds

   _____c.   Serious, but manageable through well-known software patches

   _____d.   Minor disruptive potential, and manageable through contingency planning

Overall Assessment

Taking into account your evaluations of the scenario vignettes and your answers to the questions presented above, please evaluate which of the six opening hypotheses (or combination) presented below provide the most satisfying and persuasive explanation for the Y2K outcome?

_____1. The Y2K outcome was the result of effective remediation efforts carried out by a collaborative program involving the public and private sectors.

_____2. The Y2K outcome was the result of independent private sector remediation and contingency planning efforts, with minimal involvement by governments.

_____3. The Y2K outcome was the result of government-led efforts at energizing the private sector risk assessment and technology investments in a manner that protected vital critical infrastructures from date-related disruptions.

_____4. Y2K was never a systemic threat to critical infrastructures.

_____5. The cyber-dependence of critical infrastructures was overestimated, hence reducing the significance of Y2K-related network disruptions.

_____6. The Y2K outcome is inadequately explained by any of the available models of critical infrastructure protection and infrastructure interdependencies; any final judgments should be withheld.

_____7. Other explanations

_____

_____

_____

_____

Relating Y2K to CIP Research and Development

The workshop introduction and methodology materials began with a statement of six hypotheses for explaining the relationship of the Y2K experience to critical infrastructure protection. Critical infrastructure protection differs importantly from the Y2K phenomenon in that CIP problems seldom represent date-certain events, have relatively less well-known (or at least, only partially predictable) risk exposure in critical systems, and are by their very nature subject to potential exploitation by attackers that are difficult to detect.

This part of the workshop asks participants to take the insights regarding system infrastructure interdependencies, information-sharing issues, and organizational issues collected during Part One and apply them to an evaluation of the importance of Y2K for enhancement of capabilities for CIP contingencies. The questions and subject matrix that follow ask for a more detailed discussion of concepts, processes, software, or procedures developed in the Y2K domain that may have relevance for continuing CIP efforts.

The columns in the subject matrix are designed to address areas where developments may have taken place in technical, organizational/institutional, and risk assessment categories during Y2K preparations. In order of presentation, these are:

- Computing technologies – new areas of technical research illuminated by the remediation of large and complex software systems

- Tool creation – new software and hardware tools created to manage, remediate, or mitigate Y2K software problems

- Information-sharing processes – new or revised information-sharing processes and channels utilized to communicate data on Y2K solutions, system or infrastructure remediation status, public and private sector shared learning on Y2K experiences

- Risk assessment models and approaches – new or revised risk assessment approaches (plans, programs, software, or methodologies) that were developed during the Y2K rollover

A parallel set of functional areas is also presented in the matrix, deriving from categories used by the White House Office of Science and Technology Policy to coordinate the U.S. government's CIP R&D agenda. These categories are introduced below.

- Threat/vulnerability/risk assessment – focuses on assessments, metrics, modeling and simulation, and test beds

- System protection – covers physical and cyber protection of individual systems; programs under this label include encryption, network security products, reliability and security of computing systems, and physical barriers

- Intrusion monitoring and response – detection and provision of immediate responses to infrastructure intrusions and attacks; programs include network intrusion detection, information assurance technologies, mobile code and agents, network defensive technologies, and explosives detection devices

- Reconstitution – concentrates on technologies required to reconstitute and restore critical infrastructures after serious disruptions; programs include risk management studies and tools, system survivability technologies, and consequence management tools

Evaluating the value of progress achieved during Y2K that may have some applicability to ongoing CIP concerns is critical to ensuring that the lessons learned from the rollover are not lost. The matrix and questions that follow seek to capture a portion of that experience as a means of focusing discussion on CIP research and development areas.

	Potential CIP Solutions/Capability Improvements			
Functional areas	Computing technologies (hardware and software)	Tool creation	Information-sharing processes	Risk assessment models and approaches
Threat/vulnerability/ risk assessment				
System protection				
Intrusion monitoring and response				
Reconstitution				

Y2K-CIP Linkages

The relationship posited between CIP and Y2K is directly related to initial assessments of the Y2K outcome. In many ways Y2K is more appropriately viewed as a compound event, with technical, procedural, geographic, and economic (not to mention political) features. Thematic links between Y2K and CIP can be discerned from the common subject matter—networked computing and communications resources delivering services or support to critical industrial, public service, or business applications—and from the risk assessment and contingency planning efforts synonymous in both domains.

Technologies and systems developed for Y2K to remediate systems of importance to critical infrastructure protection have the potential to offer important new capabilities for our understanding of, and responses to, threats to critical infrastructure functionality and services. An inventory of Y2K process, system, and planning innovations, with a view to their potential applicability to the enhancement of CIP capabilities, has not yet been undertaken. Beginning such an assessment process with an outline of areas where new risk assessment and/or vulnerability mitigation techniques have been developed may contribute to the translation of Y2K lessons learned into meaningful CIP capabilities.

Following the questions posed below, item four asks participants to deliberate on the technologies and process lessons derived from Y2K and to transpose them into a framework informed by the OSTP research and development resource allocation categories presented in the CIP R&D white paper. The concluding questions ask for overall impressions regarding the priority of particular areas for future research.

Mechanisms and Processes

Novel mechanisms, processes, and institutional adaptations developed during the Y2K rollover period may improve capabilities for the detection of system vulnerabilities—either deliberately introduced or the result of programming errors. From this perspective, please respond to the questions posed below.

1. What new assessment, planning, or response tools and/or information-sharing mechanisms were created during the Y2K remediation and rollover period?

_____

_____

_____

_____

_____

_____

_____

_____

2. What key systems or technologies targeted for Y2K remediation/contingency planning and response are most critical to the maintenance or enhancement of CIP capabilities?

_____

_____

_____

_____

_____

_____

_____

_____

3. What benefits, if any, did your company or organization obtain from its participation in Y2K watch center and information fusion activities?

_____

_____

_____

_____

_____

_____

_____

_____

4. Please define what you feel is an appropriate matrix of key computing technologies, information-sharing mechanisms, and risk assessment models against the prevailing OSTP CIP R&D functional categories.

_____

_____

_____

_____

_____

_____

_____

_____

5. Please give your ranking of the top four priority areas for CIP R&D activity identified in the matrix developed above.

1. _____

2. _____

3. _____

4. _____

Bibliography

Books

Alberts, Christopher, Sandra Behrens, Richard Pethia, and William Wilson. *Operationally Critical Threat, Asset, and Vulnerability Evaluation (Octave) Framework,* Version 1.0. Pittsburgh, PA: Software Engineering Institute, Carnegie Mellon University, 1999.

Alic, John A., Lewis M. Branscomb, Harvey Brooks, Ashton B. Carter, and Gerald L. Epstein. *Beyond Spinoff: Military and Commercial Technologies in a Changing World.* Cambridge, MA: Harvard University Press, 1992.

Allen, Julia, et al. *Security for Information Technology Service Centers.* Pittsburgh, PA: Software Engineering Institute, Carnegie Mellon University, 1998.

_____. *State of the Practice of Intrusion Detection Technologies.* Pittsburgh PA: Software Engineering Institute, Carnegie Mellon University, 2000.

Anderson, Robert. *Research and Development Initiatives Focused on Preventing, Detecting, and Responding to Insider MisuseoOf Critical Defense Information Systems: Results of a Three-Day Workshop.* Santa Monica, CA: RAND, CF-151-OSD, 1999.

_____. *Research Strategies To Counter the Insider Threat to Critical Information Systems.* Santa Monica, CA: RAND, IN-26204-OSD, 1999.

Anderson, Robert H., et al. *Securing the U.S. Defense Information Infrastructure: A Proposed Approach.* Santa Monica, CA: RAND, MR-993-OSD/NSA/DARPA, 1999.

Bace, Rebecca Gurley. *Intrusion Detection.* Indianapolis, IN: Macmillan, 2000.

Bagert, Donald J., Thomas B. Hilburn, Greg Hislop, Michael Lutz, Michael McCracken, and Susan Mengel. *Guidelines for Software Engineering Education,* Version 1.0. Pittsburgh, PA: Software Engineering Institute, Carnegie Mellon University, 1999.

Barbacci, M. S., P. Carriere, M. Feiler, H. Klein, T. Lipson, T. Longstaff and C. Weinstock. *Steps in an Architecture Tradeoff Analysis Method: Quality Attribute Models and Analysis.* Pittsburgh, PA: Software Engineering Institute, Carnegie Mellon University, 1998.

Capell, Peter. *Analysis of Courses of Information and Network System Security and Survivability.* Pittsburgh, PA: Software Engineering Institute, Carnegie Mellon University, 1998. Also available at http://www.sei.edu/Publication/Documents/99.Reports/99sr006/99sr006abstract.html.

Coffman, Edward G., Jr., and Peter J. Denning. *Operating Systems Theory,* Englewood Cliffs, NJ: Prentice Hall, 1973.

Denning, Dorothy E. *Cryptography and Data Security.* Reading, MA: Addison-Wesley, 1983.

_____. *Information Warfare and Security,* Reading, MA: ACM Press/Addison-Wesley, 1999.

Denning, Dorothy E., and Peter J. Denning, eds. *Internet Besieged: Countering Cyberspace Scofflaws.* New York: ACM Press, 1998.

Denning, Peter J. *Modeling Reality.* Research Institute for Advanced Computer Science, NASA Ames Research Center, 1990.

_____. *Stopping Computer Crimes.* Research Institute for Advanced Computer Science, NASA Ames Research Center, 1991.

_____. *Threats and Countermeasures for Network Security.* Research Institute for Advanced Computer Science, NASA Ames Research Center, 1993.

Denning, Peter J., ed. *Computers Under Attack: Intruders, Worms, and Viruses,* Reading, MA: Addison-Wesley, 1990.

_____. *Talking Back to the Machine: Computers and Human Aspiration.* Berlin, Germany: Springer-Verlag, 1998.

Denning, Peter J., and Robert M. Metcalfe. *Beyond Calculation: The Next Fifty Years of Computing.* Berlin, Germany: Springer-Verlag, 1997.

Ellison, B., D. A. Fisher, R. C. Linger, H. F. Lipson, T. Longstaff, and N. R. Menad. *Survivable Network Systems: An Emerging Discipline.* Pittsburgh, PA: Software Engineering Institute Technical Report No. CMU/SEI-97-TR-013, Carnegie Mellon University, 1997.

Ellison, Robert, Richard Linger, and Nancy Mead. *Case Study in Survivable Network System Analysis.* Pittsburgh, PA: Software Engineering Institute, Carnegie Mellon University, 1998.

Firth, R., G. Ford, B. Fraiser, J. Kochmar, S. Konda, J. Richael, D. Simmel, and L. Cunningham. *Detecting Signs of Intrusion in Cert.* Pittsburgh, PA: Software Engineering Institute, Carnegie Mellon University, 2000.

Fithen, Williams, et al. *Deploying Firewalls.* Pittsburgh, PA: Software Engineering Institute, Carnegie Mellon University, 1999.

Ford, Gary. *1991 SEI Report on Graduate Software Engineering Education.* Pittsburgh, PA: Software Engineering Institute, Carnegie Mellon University, 1991.

Ford, Gary, et al. *Securing Network Servers.* Pittsburgh, PA: Software Engineering Institute, Carnegie Mellon University, 1999.

The Foreign Y2K Experience: Lessons Learned and Implications for Critical Infrastructure. McLean, VA: SAIC, 2000.

Fossum, Donna, et al., *Discovery and Innovation: Federal Research and Development Activities in Fifty States, The District of Columbia, and Puerto Rico.* Santa Monica, CA: RAND, MR-1194, 2000.

Kochmar, John, et al. *Preparing to Detect Signs of Intrusion.* Pittsburgh, PA: Software Engineering Institute, Carnegie Mellon University, 1998.

_____. *Responding to Intrusions.* Pittsburgh, PA: Software Engineering Institute, Carnegie Mellon University, 1998.

Laswell, Barbara, Derek Simmel, and Sandra Behrens. *Information Assurance Curriculum and Certification: State of the Practice.* Pittsburgh, PA: Software Engineering Institute, Carnegie Mellon University, 1999.

Libicki, Martin. *Information Technology Standards: Quest for the Common Byte,* Boston, MA: Digital Press, Butterworth-Heinemann, 1995.

Little, Richard G., Paul B. Pattak, and Wayne A. Schroeder, eds. *Use of Underground Facilities to Protect Critical Infrastructures: Summary of a Workshop.* Washington, DC: National Academy Press, 1998.

Longstaff, Thomas, et al. "Security of the Internet." *The Froelich/Kent Encyclopedia of Telecommunications,* Volume 15. New York: Marcel Dekker, Inc., 1977: 231–255.

Molander, Roger, et al. *Strategic Information Warfare Rising.* Santa Monica, CA: RAND, MR-964-OSD, 1998.

Northcutt, Stephen, and Judy Novak. *Network Intrusion Detection: An Analyst's Handbook.* 2nd ed. Indianapolis, IN: New Riders, 2000.

Perlman, Radia. *Interconnections Second Edition: Bridges, Routers, Switches, and Internetworking Protocols.* Reading, MA: Addison-Wesley, 2000.

Perrow, Charles. *Normal Accidents: Living with High Risk Technologies.* New York: Basic Books, 1984.

Power, Richard. *Current and Future Danger: A CSI Primer on Computer Crime and Information Warfare.* San Francisco, CA: Computer Security Institute, 1998.

Rogers, Lawrence R. *Rlogin(1): The Untold Story.* Pittsburgh, PA: Software Engineering Institute, Carnegie Mellon University, 1998.

Schwartau, Winn. *Cybershock: Surviving Hackers, Phreakers, Identity Thieves, Internet Terrorists and Weapons of Mass Destruction.* New York: Thunder's Mouth Press, 2000.

_____. *Information Warfare: Chaos on the Electronic Superhighway.* New York: Thunder's Mouth Press, 1994.

_____. *Information Warfare: Cyberterrorism: Protecting Your Personal Security In The Electronic Age.* 2nd ed. New York: Thunder's Mouth Press, 1996.

Schwartau, Winn, and Chris Goggans. *The Complete Internet Business Toolkit.* New York: Van Nostrand Reinhold, 1996.

Simmel, Derek, et al. *Securing Desktop Workstations.* Pittsburgh, PA: Software Engineering Institute, Carnegie Mellon University, 1999.

Smith, Dennis B., Hausi A. Muller, and Scott R. Tilley. *The Year 2000 Problem: Issues and Implications.* Software Engineering Institute, Carnegie Mellon University, 1997.

West-Brown, Moria J., Don Stikvoort, and Klaus-Peter Kossakowski. *Handbook for Computer Security Incident Response Teams (CSIRTs).* Pittsburgh, PA: Software Engineering Institute, Carnegie Mellon University, 1998.

Journals, Periodicals and Newspapers

Barnes, Bruce H. "Computer Security Research: A British Perspective." *IEEE Software* 15.5 (1998): 30–33.

Barrett, Daniel J. "Statistics and Computer Crime." *Computer* 29 (1996): 14.

Bequai, August. "High-Tech Security and the Failings of President Clinton's Commission on Critical Infrastructure Protection." *Computers and Security* 17.1 (1998): 19.

Boulanger, A. "Catapults and Grappling Hooks: The Tools and Techniques of Information Warfare." *IBM Systems Journal* 14 (Sept/Oct 1997): 106–114.

Campen, Alan D. "National Vulnerability Intensifies as Infrastructure Reliance." *Signals* 52.11 (1998). Also available at http//www.us.net/Archive/July98/national-July.htm.

Cohen, Reuven, Keren Erez, Daniel Ben-Avraham, and Shlomo Havlin. "Resilience of the Internet to Random Breakdowns," *Physical Review Letters*, Volume 85.21 (2000): 4626–4628.

"Computer Security and the Internet; Special Report." *Scientific American* 279. 4 (1998): 95–117.

Cheswick, William, Steven M. Bellovin, and Warwick Ford. "How Computer Security Works." *Scientific American* 279. 4 (1998): 106–109.

Cronin, Blaise, and Holly Crawford. "Information Warfare: Its Application in Military and Civilian Contexts." *The Information Society* 15.4 (1999): 257–263.

Crow, Patrick. "The Real Y2K Threat." *Oil & Gas Journal* 97.34 (1999): 36.

Durst, Robert, Terrence Champion, and Brian Witten. "Testing and Evaluation: Computer Intrusion Detection Systems." *Communications of the ACM* 42.7 (1999): 53–61.

Frincke, Deborah. "Balancing Cooperation and Risk Intrusion Detection." *ACM Transactions on Information and System Security (Tissec)* 3.1 (2000): 1–29.

Ghosh, Anup K., and Jeffrey M. Voas. "Inoculation Software for Survivability." *Communications of the ACM* 42.7 (1999): 38–44.

Gips, Michael A. "News and Trends." *Security Management* 43.9 (1999): 15.

Godau, Ralph I. "The Changing Face of Infrastructure Management." *Systems Engineering* 2.4 (1999): 226–236.

Graham-Rowe, Duncan. "To the Virtual Barricades." *New Scientist* 163.2204 (1999): 18–19.

Greenwald, Judy. "Y2K May Cost U.S. $50 Billion." *Business Insurance* 32.18 (1998).

Harrington, David. "Leave Y2K Remediation to the Experts: Clinical Engineers." *Journal of Clinical Engineering* 24.4 (1999): 219.

Irvine, Cynthia E. "Challenges in Computer Security Education." *IEEE Software* 14 (1997): 110–111.

Jung, Changduk, Ingoo Han, and Bomil Suh. "Risk Analysis for Electronic Commerce Using Case-Base Reasoning." *International Journal of Intelligent SystemsIn Accounting, Finance & Management* 8.1 (1999): 61–73.

Lipinski, Tomas A. "Information Warfare, American Style." *IEEE Technology & Society Magazine* 18.1 (1999): 10–19.

Mann, Paul. "'Asymmetrical' Threats New Military Watchword." *Aviation Week & Space Technology* 148.7 (1998): 55.

Mann, Paul. "Officials Grapple with 'Undeterrable' Terrorism." *Aviation Week & Space Technology* 149.2 (1998): 67.

Marcoccia, Louis J. "Building Infrastructure for Fixing the Year 2000 Bug: A Case Study." *Journal of Software Maintenance: Research and Practice* 10.5 (1998): 333–325.

McGee, Marianna Kolbasuk. "Y2K: Work to Do—Study Shows Testing and Remediation Efforts Lagging." *Information Week*, August 17 (1998): 24.

McGuire, David. "Power Grids Ready for Y2K." *Newsbytes* August 9 (1999). Also available at http://www.computeruser.com/Newtoday/99/08/09/News7.html.

Meeuwsen, J. J., W. Kling, and Waga Ploem. "The Influence of Protection System Failures and Preventive Maintenance on Protection Systems in Distribution Systems." *IEEE Transactions on Power Delivery* 12 (1997): 125–133.

Miyawaki, Raisuke. *The Fight Against Cyberterrorism : A Japanese View* CSIS, 1999. 23 February 2000, http://www.csis.org/html/Sp990629miyawaki.html.

"Most Small Chemical Companies in Four States Not Y2K Ready, Study Finds." *PR Newswire* October 22 (1999): 12.

Mussington, David. "Throwing the Switch in Cyberspace." *Jane's Intelligence Review* 8.7 (1996): 331–334.

Neumann, Peter G. "Protecting the Infrastructures." *Communications of the ACM* 41 (1998): 128.

Nordwall, Bruce D. "Cyber Threats Place Infrastructure at Risk." *Aviation Week & Space Technology* 146 June 30 (1997): 51.

Panda, Brajendra, and Joseph Giordano. "Defensive Information Warfare." *Communications of the ACM* 42.7 (1999): 30–32.

Perry, Tekla S. "Checking Up on Y2K." *IEEF Spectrum* 36.7 (1999): 61–70.

Puttre, Michael. "Security Technology Frisks Without Fingers." *Design News* 51 (1996): 29–30.

Schneider, Fred. "Enforceable Security Policies." *The ACM Transactions on Information and System Security* 3.1 (2000): 30–50.

Schneier, Bruce. "Attack Trees." *Dr. Dobbs Journal*, December 1999, http://www.ddj.com/Articles/1999/9912/9912a/9912a.htm.

Scott, William B. "High States Space ISC2 Program Attracts Multi-Skill Bidders." *Aviation Week & Space Technology* 151.20 (1999): 101–102.

Smith, George. "How Vulnerable Is Our Interlinked Infrastructure? An Electronic Pearl Harbor? Not Likely—The Government's Evidence About U.S. Vulnerability to Cyber Attack Is Shaky at Best." *Issues in Science and Technology* 15.1 (1998). Also available at http://205.130.185.236/Issues/15.1/Smith.htm.

Spinellis, Diomidis. "Reflection as a Mechanism for Software Integrity Verification." *The ACM Transactions on Information and System Security* 3.1 (2000): 51–62.

West-Brown, Morai, and Julia Allen. "From Y2K to Security Improvement: A Critical Transition." *Security Matters*, 2.3 (September 1999). 14 January 2000 http://interactive.sei.cmu.edu/Columns/Security_Matters/1999/September/Security.Sep99.htm.

Yalla, Murty V.V.S, Everett C. Fennell, and M Bajpai. "Application of Multifunction Generator Protection Systems." *IEEE Transactions on Power Delivery* 14.4 (1999): 1285–1294.

Government Documents and Miscellaneous Items

Borchgrave, Arnaud De. "On The Y2K Crisis." CSIS, 1998. 23 February 2000 http://www.csis.org/goc/ao981013.html.

Brock, Jack L., Jr. "Critical Infrastructure Protection: Comments on the National Plan for Information Systems Protection." Washington, DC: U.S. General Accounting Office, Hearing Before the Subcommittee on Technology, Terrorism and Government Information, Committee on the Judiciary, U.S. Senate, 2000.

_____. "Critical Infrastructure Protection: Fundamental Improvements Needed to Assure Security of Federal Operations." Washington, DC: U.S. General Accounting Office, Hearing Before the Subcommittee on Technology, Terrorism and Government Information, Committee on the Judiciary, U.S. Senate, 2000.

Commercial Perspectives on Information Assurance Research. Vol. P-3359, Ft. Belvoir: Institute for Defense Analyses, 1998.

Committee to Review DoD C4I Plans And Programs. "Information Systems Security," Chapter 3 in *Realizing the Potential of C4I: Fundamental Challenges,* Washington, DC: National Research Council, National Academy Press, 1999, 289.

Defending America's Cyberspace: National Plan for Information Systems Protection, Version 1.0. Washington, DC, January 2000.

Denning, Dorothy E., and Herbert S. Lin. "Rights and Responsibilities of Participants in Networked Communities." Steering Committee on Rights and Responsibilities of Participants in Networked Communities, Computer Science and Telecommunications Board, Commission on Physical Sciences, Mathematics, and Applications, Washington, DC: National Research Council, National Academy Press, 1994.

Ellis, James, David Fisher, Thomas Longstaff, Linda Pesante, and Richard Pethia. "Report to the President's Commission on Critical Infrastructure Protection." Pittsburgh, PA: Software Engineering Institute, 1997.

Ellison, Robert J., David A. Fisher, Richard C. Linger, Howard F. Lipson, Thomas A. Longstaff, and Nancy R. Mead. "Protecting Critical Systems in Unbounded Networks." *SEI Interactive: Security Matters*, 24 December 1999. 1 January 2000 http://Interactive.sei.cmu.edu/columns/security_matters/1999/December/security.Dec99.htm.

Gennaro, R., and S. Micali. "Verifiable Secret Sharing as Secure Computation." In *Advances in Cryptology—Eurocrypt '95*. In L. C. Guillou and J.-J. Quisquater, eds. *Lecture Notes in Computer Science* 921 (1995): 168–182.

"Intensive Preparation for Y2K Rollover Produces Long-Term Benefits for Global Air-Transport," January/February 2000. 23 February 2000 http://Www.Icao.Int/Icao/En/Jr/5501_Up.htm.

Libicki, Martin. *What Is Information Warfare?* Washington, DC: National Defense University, ACIS Paper, 3 August 1995.

North American Electric Reliability Council. *Critical Infrastructure Inter-Dependency Contingency Planning: Electricity – Telecommunications – Natural Gas – Oil – Transportation – Inter-Industry Technical Group Report of the Inter-Industry Contingency Planning Task Force*, Washington, DC: GPO, 1999.

_____. *Preparing the Electric Power Systems of North America for Transition to the Year 2000: A Status Report Update – Third Quarter 1999*. Washington, DC: GPO, 1999.

_____. *Year 2000 Critical Infrastructure Inter-Industry Contingency Planning: Electricity, Communications, Gas, Oil, Coal, and Transportation*. Washington, DC: GPO, 1999.

_____. *Year 2000 Interoperability Test Evaluation Report*. Washington, DC: GPO, 1999.

President's Commission on Critical Infrastructure Protection (PCCIP). *Critical Foundations: Protecting America's Infrastructures*, Washington, DC, 1997. Also available at http://www.pccip.gov/.

Raymond, Eric. *The Cathedral and the Bazaar*, as excerpted on the web, 1998 http://www.Firstmonday.Dk/Issues/Issue3_3/Raymond/.

U.S. General Accounting Office, *Year 2000 Computing Challenge: Lessons Can Be Applied to Other Management Challenges* (GAO/AIMD-00-290, September 2000).

_____, Accounting and Information Management Division, *Year 2000 Computing Challenge: Readiness of FBI's National Instant Criminal Background Check System Can Be Improved*. (GAO-1999).

_____, Accounting and Information Management Division, *Y2K Computing Challenge: Day One Planning and Operations Guide*.

_____, Accounting and Information Management Division, *Year 2000 Computing Crisis: An Assessment Guide*. (GAO-1997).

U.S. Senate, Commission on Critical Infrastructure Protection, Hearing Before the Senate Committee on the Judiciary Subcommittee on Technology, Terrorism and Government

Information. "Critical Information Infrastructure Protection: The Threat Is Real." Washington, DC, 1999.

_____, Subcommittee on Technology, Terrorism, and Government Information of the Committee on the Judiciary. "Critical Infrastructure Protection: Toward a New Policy Directive." Washington, DC: GPO 1998, 163.

_____, Hearing Before the Subcommittee on Technology, Terrorism and Government Information Committee on the Judiciary. "Cyber Attack: The National Protection Plan and Its Privacy Implications." Washington, DC, 2000.

_____, Hearing Before the Subcommittee on Technology, Terrorism, and Government Information of the Committee on the Judiciary. "The Nation at Risk: Report of the President's Commission on Critical Infrastructure Protection." Washington, DC, 1997, 72.

_____, Hearing Before the Subcommittee on Technology, Terrorism, and Government Information. "The Encryption Debate: Criminals, Terrorists and the Security Needs of Business and Industry," 1997, Washington, DC, ICAO Year 2000 [Cited 02/23/00 2000]. Available from http://www.icao.int/Y2K/.

Willemssen , Joel C. "Year 2000 Computing Challenge: Leadership and Partnerships Result in Limited Rollover Disruptions." Washington, DC: United States General Accounting Office, Hearing Before the Subcommittee on Government Management, Information and Technology, Committee on Government Reform, and the Subcommittee on Technology, Committee on Science, House of Representatives, January 27, 2000.

_____. "Year 2000 Computing Challenge: Noteworthy Improvements in Readiness But Vulnerabilities Remain." Washington, DC: United States General Accounting Office, Hearing Before the Subcommittee on Technology, Committee on Science, and the Subcommittee on Government Management, Information, and Technology, Committee on Government Reform, House of Representatives, 1999.

_____. "Year 2000 Computing Crisis: Readiness Status of the Department of Health and Human Services." Washington, DC: United States General Accounting Office, Hearing Before the Subcommittee on Government Management, Information and Technology, Committee on Government Reform, House of Representatives, 1999.